BREAKING ECHOES

Heather Stoker

EABooks Publishing
Your Partner In Publishing

Name: Heather Stoker
Title: Breaking Echoes
ISBN: 978-1-953114-03-7
LCCN: 2021918830
Subjects: 1. FAMILY & RELATIONSHIPS/ Abuse / Child Abuse
2. POETRY /Subjects & Themes / General
3. SELF HELP / Adult Children of Substance Abusers

Interior Design by Darryl Bennett
All interior images are personal photos of the author or from family photo albums.
Front Cover Design by Nathan Stoker. Image from family photo album.
Back Cover Designed by Robin Black

Published by EA Books Publishing, a division of
Living Parables of Central Florida, Inc. a 501c3

EABooksPublishing.com

"The eyes are perhaps the only
reliable barometers of emotion,
instruments of empathy
and windows of truth."
—Anonymous

Table of Contents

Author's Note

It has taken me fifty-five years to come to terms with my early childhood, to make sense of the trauma, abuse, and aftermath. I have chosen to tell my story now, because my perpetrators or abusers have passed. I now no longer feel the need to protect their identity or keep their secrets.

In my effort to come forward, I know that by breaking the silence, I will be heard and in doing so, this will be therapeutic in my healing and ability to move forward with my life.

Another reason I've decided to write my story is to release others from their own individual suffering, those who can relate to my life. It serves to validate them as survivors, enabling them to find their voice and be heard. It can also serve to suppress the shame or guilt they may wrongly carry in their hearts for so long.

It won't be an easy story to write, as it does entail releasing painful details that living family members were not aware of. But in the end my efforts are to bring closure to this part of my life and to give hope and inspiration to others.

At times, I will be remembering thoughts and situations from a child's point of view. It can be confusing for some to read, but I will do my best to clarify and explain it. No matter how confusing this chaotic, dysfunctional beginning was, it was my start in life. Regardless of our scars, they can heal and you can move on to become a productive person in society. I am now a mother of two, a Registered Nurse and my life is worth living each and every day.

I am thankful for my boys who have always stood beside me and my sister, Kathy Hebb, who has always been my protector since the start of life and whose memoir also fills in the details I may have forgotten as she is three years older than myself. She has given me her blessings to come forward to write my story and share hers. I am forever grateful to her always.

Chapter 1
The Beginning

My sister, age nine and I, age six were excited to be boarding an airplane for the first time. We were traveling with a DCF (Department of Children and Families) lady who accompanied us to the terminal to board a plane headed to Canada. In our mind we thought we were going for a visit to meet our grandparents, but that visit would turn into twelve years before I'd return to Tampa, Florida.

Let me begin by telling you about our early childhood years, while we were growing up with our biological parents. My sister and I were born in Tampa, Florida. Our normal life was turbulent, chaotic, unpredictable, and without routine or structure. Both of our parents were alcoholics. My father was a mechanic by trade and my mother a homemaker.

My father worked hard and left early in the morning, arriving home later in the evening. He'd typically go to the bar after work, before he would make it home. My mother took care of us during the day, but many times she didn't provide basic good care due to her alcohol abuse.

I can now look back and remember many unsettling things. Once I became a parent myself, I really learned fast about the many sacrifices you make to be a good mother. Unfortunately, my mother cared more about the drink than being a responsible parent. And my dad wasn't any better. He chose to be an absent dad and spent his time in bars after work, instead of coming home to us.

I can't really say that I bonded with my parents during the six years that I had known them. I can also say that my sister never did either. How can you love someone who doesn't appreciate you, compliment you or take care of you when you're just a child?

Meals were provided sometimes, not always. It depended on whether my mother had the money to buy food, or if she had used it to buy booze. Also, if she had passed out on the couch from drinking all day meals were not prepared. My sister soon took on the role of my mom, watching over me and protecting me the best that she knew how. Sometimes that meant picking avocados from a tree in the backyard and eating them to fill our hungry stomachs. It's funny, because for years I never ate them but just recently started buying them. After calling my sister, she informed me of this memory and enlightened me on this being one of the foods that probably kept us alive.

There were times when we were left at home locked inside and there was no food, just an empty fridge. My sister Kathy would take a chair and push it over to look in the freezer. She'd find a package of frozen hamburger and after it started defrosting, we'd devour it. We were so hungry.

This was our life. We accepted it and accepted our parents as is, we didn't know any better. I learned at an early age to steal, as my mother would take me in the store with her. I'd be sitting in the shopping cart and she would pick up and put items in her purse. We'd pay for the few things she had gathered, but not everything. Reflecting back, I wondered if the grocery money my dad gave her was spent on liquor or drinking at the bar, leaving her little or no money to buy food for us.

It was not uncommon for my mom to load us in the car and visit the bar. We'd be locked in the car for hours at a time awaiting her return. I'm sure this is why to this day, I don't like being in a room with the door closed. It's always uncomfortable when seeing my doctor and they close the door behind them. I always have to tell them, "Please leave the door open." If not, I can feel myself getting anxious, almost like a panic attack, my heart starts racing and I feel like I can't breathe. It's a very uncomfortable feeling, almost like I'm going to die.

As we grew older, it became almost a ritual that both my sister and I would be picked up by the police and be accompanied home in the wee hours of the morning. We'd take late night walks looking in shop windows at bicycles that we wished we could have. Since there was no supervision by my parents, we did as we pleased. We didn't realize the danger we were in. Anything could of happened to us, anyone could have taken us, abused, or sold us into the black market for sex trafficking. I feel now that an angel must have been watching over us, protecting us from harm.

Myself, about 3 and my sister age 6.
So long ago, and yet I can see the innocence and I'm
forever grateful for my protector, my sister.

Reflection

As a child I felt powerless, introverted and shy,
always felt different, but didn't know why...
Suppressing feelings, I kept deep secrets inside...
They slowly festered, and I had nowhere to hide...
the silence was defining and killing me inside...
then grown with children of my own,
I knew I must face my demons straight on,
to be no longer a prisoner,
I chose to heal and move on
to find my voice with words to be clear
would be my healer, my truth, my dear.
I built up my armor from years ago,
from what I have endured, I know...
I count, I'm here,
to stand for those who live in fear...
abuse, neglect is wrong in every way
I am living proof there is salvation today.

Chapter 2
Early Childhood

What are these reflections meant to be? The dictionary says the word reflection means: something reflected, as light, radiant heat, sound, or an image.

Reflection

My sister sits on the floor quietly at play,
brushing her dolls hair and dreaming away...
unknowing and trusting, she relied on you,
but doesn't understand the bad things you do...
darkness brings creatures that come out at night,
they don't hide in closets or stay out of sight.
You won't find them hiding under your bed,
but they enter your nightmares instead.
They live within your dwelling,
seem kind in a weird sort of way,
but really they are monsters just coming out to play.

I'm five years old in this photo,
my sister eight playing doctor and
patient in imaginary play.

Survivors of sexual abuse, we were there for each other ... and always will be. My past comes with pain, but I don't let it stain my present. There is healing when you break your silence and tell your story by speaking the truth. As I write my book, I hope others can break their silence to heal and recover. You can prevail and go on to live a full, productive life, find strength in yourself, and believe you are deserving.

Reflection

It's as if the light has been turned on, and in doing so, the darkness is
gone, I emerged from the war, broken and screaming...
scarred, confused, alive and bleeding...
The protective shell I formed is now breaking,
there's a thirst for life I'm taking...
To find the person I should be,
your control no longer intimidates me,
it died with you to give me life,
your words no longer cut me like a knife...
worthiness, value, identity stripped from me,
all that is gone, I'm finally free.
My heart is healing, a rebirth you might say...
there's life with healing; it's a brand new day.

Family addiction hurts the entire family, resulting in codependency, dysfunction, and destruction. Born to parents who are alcoholics resulted in neglect, abuse, and a difficult start in life. My grandparents raised me, however my grandfather too was an alcoholic. Any person in an addiction is miserable and it eventually destroys all family dynamics, a vicious cycle. I married an alcoholic, and divorced him after twenty-three years and two boys later. Life begins when you can recognize a pattern and finally break it. Two of my abusers have since died and now I feel strong enough to come forward to tell my story, in an effort to reach others who are or have been afflicted with the pain of living with an addicted person. Be strong and never give up hope, you are loved and there is life after recovery, peace can be restored to your life again.

Reflection

Look deep within my eyes, my wisdom dwells there...
it borders my face along with my hair.
It shows deep in lines on my face, took years to form,
to never be erased...
many memories of childhood have formed me,
sculpted me to be here today, never forgotten, just a nightmare away...
Dark places were there...
I searched to be sought...
to be found alive, for life again I fought.
Empty holes of despair in my heart lived there...
but I never gave in...
I looked for the light to pull me back in again...
music and writing gave me a way to cope,
and in my teen years I clung to hope.
Sometimes it got lonely, I wished I was dead,
but there was always something that changed my mind instead...
I remember those days I'll never forget,
but acceptance is peace now...
my demons are dead,
they no longer live...
just still in my head.

My one and only sister, age sixteen, moved out; it wasn't planned, it just happened one day. She went through hell and survived, only to be told she had to leave. I was devastated, I was 14. Loss is never easy; I lost my parents and now my big sister. It would be months to a year before I would see or hear from her again ... That was a difficult time for me ... I remember. Our hearts are healing and we will always be there for each other ... I will write more in my book on this time in my life ... Love you, Sis

Chapter 3
Family Addiction

My father wasn't home much, but he was the disciplinary person as he would use his belt on us for misbehaving. He really kept to himself, a mechanic by trade during the day and then bar drinking and misbehaving at night, but never in our presence. He'd arrive home in the wee hours of the morning or not at all.

If he arrived home drunk there were sometimes arguments with my mother, who was also drunk. One time, my father took out a knife and threatend my mother, my sister stood between them. They eventually calmed down and the argument didn't go any further that night.

My mother put her addiction to alcohol first. We were just there to contend with. She preferred hard liquor and would do anything to get it. She would turn "tricks" or prostitute to get her booze. She'd take us in a car and drive us to a man's house and leave us locked in the car. It would seem like hours and hours before she'd come back to us with her pay, so she could buy more liquor. She seldom spent the money on food at the grocery store to feed us.

Another memory my sister recalls, one night when I was just a baby in my crib, I started crying loudly. My sister came running in to see a man crawling through my window, thinking it was my mother's bedroom. Kathy grabbed me out of the crib and brought me to her room. She doesn't remember my father being there, but my mom was in her bedroom waiting for the strange man to arrive. My mom was a "lady of the night" just another trick for her. As my mother's drinking started spiraling out of control, so did her actions and judgement. In her sick state of mind, she cared about finding her addiction only, even at the cost of her daughters' innocence. Kathy remembers my mom passed out on the bed and the next moment Kathy had a man's penis in her mouth. She was about seven and crying "Why was he peeing in my mouth?" This trauma would follow her later once she became married and in an intimate time with her husband. Kathy would resent, hate, and be disgusted with her biological mother for twenty years before she would come to terms with her feelings to forgive her.

In retrospect, I remember my parents never showing love for each other. There was never hand holding, kissing, hugging, or any displays of affection. I can say for myself, I never felt love. In fact, there was no show of affection or admiration, no emotional attachments, or bonding. My sister Kathy would later tell me she felt the same.

Eight years later, it would be my grandmother who would say that our dad always wanted a boy, not girls. He wanted someone to hunt and fish with. I remember how hurt I felt after she had said this and he did eventually remarry after he divorced our mother and he finally had the son that he always wanted.

My father lived and grew up in Nova Scotia, Canada. He finished high school and took up mechanic work like his dad and moved to Florida when he was twenty. His aunt Melita lived there and encouraged him to move down. He met my mother in a bar and when he married her she was already pregnant with another man's child. I would not know this and neither would Kathy until eight years later when it was revealed in a drunken outburst from my grandfather at the dinner table. I'll elaborate more on that later.

My father only went home once to Canada when he was twenty-three. My grandmother came down several times and noticed things were not good. As babies we were over the age of two and not yet potty trained. Medical care was neglected, my sister Kathy had repeated bilateral ear infections which drained down her neck; eventually this would cause her permanent ear damage that she has to this day. For myself, I was always given hand-me-down shoes that never fit properly, causing a lot of foot pain and damage. Kathy and I never wore new clothes; they were bought at thrift shops or Salvation Army, including shoes. This was the same with toys of which we had very few.

I can't say that I remember any family time together, even holidays like Christmas and Easter I don't remember. I can glance at some of the old photos we have, but still can't say there was much love or a feeling of being cared for or treasured. Kathy and I were just existing, not living.

Eventually DCF (Department of Children and Families) and CPS (Child Protective Services) did intervene and we were put in foster homes on more than one occasion. I have a vivid memory of my birthday, as my mother came to visit us and brought me an Easy Bake Oven. I could play with it for a short time, but was not allowed to make the batter or bake the cookies as the foster

My father Richard aged twenty-three (left) pictured with his dad (right)

mother wouldn't allow me. It was not good living there, we were told to eat our dinner and if not we'd never receive desert, that being an orange. I remember how upset I was, because I didn't finish my food and was sent to my room without getting my orange.

Everything was so confusing, Kathy and I had each other, but it was terrible. Our foster mom was strict. I remember she had short red hair and had no patience with us. I cried a lot, not knowing why we were there and why we couldn't go home.

Reflection:

I can smell the earth with the rain pelting down,
drizzling it streams down the windowpane making a comforting sound...
It washes away the dirt as if to say...
everything will be clean again,
look forward to a "new day"...
Don't waste time looking back,
but don't forget the lessons learned along the way.
Be grateful you survived and look for the rainbow instead...

It follows the storm, just navigate ahead. All of us have experienced pain sometime in our life, the trick is don't let it overcome you. Take that pain and make it your motivation to change and rise above it. I survived childhood abuse, neglect, a divorce after twenty-three years of marriage … mother of two, I've worked hard to heal and become a nurse, writer, and photographer …

Don't be afraid to speak—you will heal others—don't be afraid to listen—the words can find the ones who need to hear them—don't be afraid to reach out to touch—you will feel again—don't be afraid to fall—you will rise again, stronger and better than ever before.

When we work to see the "good" that comes from the "bad" we are active and not sedentary. This brings you to a place of reasoning, of gaining growth from the experience. A negative can be a positive thing … You just have to do the work to see it. Look at the pain not as "Why does this always happen to me?" Instead ask yourself aloud and purposely, "Why has this happened for me?"

Chapter 4
The Move

On a December day, Kathy and I headed to the airport and I don't remember saying goodbye to my parents, we really didn't know what was going on. I was six and my big sister was nine, and after several times being put in foster homes, the courts decided we would be put up for adoption. It was determined that both parents were unfit to give us a safe home due to their alcoholism, neglect and abuse. There was a likelihood that we would be separated and go to separate homes. Ultimately, out grandparents agreed to raise us in Nova Scotia, Canada where we would be able to stay together. The year was 1969.

As we boarded the plane, we were excited because this was the first time we had ever flown. I was recovering from a tonsillectomy, my sister remembers. We believed we were going to visit our grandparents in Canada and so we were dressed appropriately with coats, boots, hats and mittens. Again, not knowing the reasons for such heavy clothes, we would soon find out when we finally arrived at the Halifax Airport on that stormy winter night.

At the airport, there was a taxi waiting for us. We were walked to the cab and upon doing so Kathy noticed our footprints in the snow. She got scared, shouted and pointed "Look, someone is following us!" The cab driver explained that was not the case and it calmed her down. It was dark and late when the cab pulled into the long driveway that was lined with tall pine trees on both sides.

Once the car came to a stop, the cab driver came out and opened our door to help us out. Kathy held my hand tight as we proceeded to the lighted doorway and walked up the steps. We made our way to the front door waiting as the driver knocked. As the door opened, we were greeted by our grand-mother. Soon after, hearing the commotion, my grandfather came down the stairs to meet us. We were both frightened as he made a wheezing sound as he breathed. Later we would find out he had asthma. Suddenly, my grand-mother made a move to pick me up, but Kathy quickly stood in front of me, in an effort to protect me. My grandfather commented "Isn't that cute." Then my grandmother bent down and looking at Kathy said, "It was ok." She told us that they were our grandparents and we were going to live here and told us their names, Norma and Robert.

We were both very sick when we arrived in Canada. We were treated for head lice, round worm and tape worms, and I was healing from a recent tonsillectomy. I had a scar on my left forearm. I would find out later that this was caused by a window falling on my arm as I pulled a can of toys out that were holding the window open. I was four or five at the time.

As we settled into this new environment, it was certainly different. My grandparents were strict, schedules needed to be followed. We always had chores to do. We'd wash and dry the dishes daily, also cleaning the house when asked to do so. It became routine and we got used to helping out.

We lived in a small house, maybe 700 to 800 square feet in total, includ-ing the attic space we slept in. There was one bathroom, a small kitchen with a sink and a burning stove. In the summer we used wood to burn but, in the winter, we relied on propane to heat the stove in the house.

I remember my grandmother worked hard to keep the house orderly and clean. She'd hand wash clothes in a tub and use a scrub board to clean them, rinsing and wringing them out one by one to take them outside to hang on a clothesline to dry. Whether it was summer or winter, that's how our laundry was done.

My grandmother also worked at Mrs. Jones house as the cook, house-cleaner, and helped out with the children. She went to work every day after we left for school. She'd walk three miles there and three miles back every day arriving home shortly after we did. I remember getting home from school and putting my books down to pick up the broom or mop to clean our kitchen so she wouldn't have to come home to do it. I just wanted to make things better for her.

As I remember, my grandfather stayed at home because he was fired and could no longer find work as a mechanic as his alcoholism took over his life.

Money was tight. I do remember the Salvation Army bringing us our holiday boxes at Thanksgiving and Christmas, complete with a full dinner and a toy for Kathy and me. Holidays were simple, a large cooked meal, a few gifts, most were handmade, not many things.

My grandfather could be kind when he wasn't drinking. He loved animals more than people. I say this, because he had a soft spot for them. We had hens, chickens, guinea hens, ducks, and a pet raccoon named "Honeybun", a dog named "Chops", and many cats. At one time we had 14 cats. Kathy and I loved the animals. That was one thing that made the transition easier.

The cats were constantly breeding and before you knew it, there would be a new litter born. Then Kathy and I would rush to see them before going to school. Before long, the kittens would grow bigger, but before the eyes opened, my grandfather would have to "take care of them." Litter by litter they would be disposed of. We'd hear my grandmother telling him "Its time," and that meant he'd need to drown them. I

Pictures of "Honeybun" and "Chops"

became used to seeing a large white pickle bucket brought out the night before. On that day, my grandfather would get very drunk and the arguing would continue into the night.

I remember running into the porch in the morning to look in the box to see it empty, no kittens there. Over the years, when my grandfather would return from carrying out the task, one kitten would be alive. He would tell my grandmother a story of how it crawled out after and survived, and he couldn't submerge them again. I think that he hated to do this, but my grandmother insisted, as we couldn't afford to keep all those cats. I'm not sure why they didn't get them spayed or neutered, but most likely it was the cost. It always saddened me to see them go.

It would be my grandfather's love and compassion for animals that would be his only redeeming quality and I followed in his footsteps becoming an avid animal lover too.

Reflection

A gaze upon a yellow rose today,
bursting with buds as if to say...
I've managed to bloom without little care,
and despite the neglect I'm here to share,
an abundance of beauty for your eyes to see,
it doesn't really matter what you did to me...
I will survive to shine,
to be your window to cope,
when things go wrong,
I'm always here to cast a sliver of hope my dear...
and teach you the lessen that can't be taught,
that you won't understand as a small child to see...
that who you are and what you do,
will be the most important thing to me...
your value, strength, and promise to be,
I know you can make it and set your soul free.

Dedicated to my grandmother, Norma Hebb, also known as my mother who passed away May 2002. She only wanted the best for us. She was kind but strict, a hard worker and still managed to take care of my sister and me. We watched her struggle, and suffer at the hands of her abuser, my grandfather. She provided and protected us the best way she knew how, but that wasn't enough. Upon my grandfather's passing, she finally found peace. Only then, did I tell her about our own abuse from him. She was an extraordinary person, the most influential woman in my life. I will always be grateful for the lessons she taught me. To never give up, to be strong, to persevere and to always survive. Always and forever missed, Heather and Kathy.

Norma Hebb (left)
pictured with her grandson Ryan (right)

In Memory of Norma Hebb
1919-2002

Chapter 5
Life on the Farm

Still these reflections come to me. And to my sister. Reflections upon reflections, some cold as ice, others radiating with heart. Some thrown forward, others bent back, other's forming an image, and still others a result of someone's actions. Some like a mirror, others like an optical telescope.

I remember life on the farm was always busy. A normal routine for my grandfather was to get up and take care of the animals; chickens, ducks, dogs and cats that needed to be fed, their water dishes and trays cleaned and topped off with water. I remembered the first time my grandfather reached under the hens to collect eggs and in doing so, took one egg, poked a hole in the bottom and sucked it down in one swallow.

My grandfather pictured with the ducks

My grandfather pictured with a chicken and our Basset Hound dog "Chops"

I somehow always remembered that sound whenever my grandmother took to baking and cooking, which was often. Kathy and I loved my grandmother's baking. She always made the best cookies and sweetbreads and pies. We'd wait patiently until she was finished, then we'd rush to lick the bowls, spoon and mixing utensils clean. Some of the farm eggs were hard boiled and put in a pickle jar. This was one of the foods we'd find in our lunchboxes at school.

I don't remember much about my early years in school. I know we never missed school, unless we were very sick or had a fever. I was very shy and kept to myself, Kathy was more outgoing than me. We were always clean and were dressed appropriately. Our clothes were always used or bought at thrift or consignment shops. New shoes were bought at the store, and maybe underwear and socks.

I remember our dress clothes for church. I loved to wear the frilly dresses and pretty dress shoes. Kathy and I always had to go to church every Sunday. However, our grandparents never did. We went to many different churches, Baptist, United, and Pentecostal and we walked there, just as we did to go to school to wait at the bus stop.

Sunday drives would be with Uncle Wallace and Aunt Helen. I can recall how sick I'd feel, I always got motion sickness and headaches when we drove for a long period of time. My favorite thing would be when we stopped to eat ice cream at the ice cream shop. Kathy and I loved that.

It became almost normal for us to hear our grandparents arguing. My grandfather would start drinking early in the day, and as the hours went by, he'd get intoxicated. My grandmother would be so upset when she'd get home and take one look at him. She knew right away; he was drunk and as the night wore on my grandfather's temperament would worsen.

We'd hear him belittling her, putting her down, accusing her of cheating, just screaming and being a horrible person. We were frightened when he'd get pushy and lash out to grab my grandmother's arm to hurt her. I can remember looking down the air vent from our bedroom in the attic to watch as the arguing continued into the night.

I was afraid of what could happen as he drank himself into stupor. He'd light a cigarette and so many times my grandmother would be worried that he was going to burn down the house. One of the biggest aggravations for my grandmother was how he was getting his liquor, who was getting it for him. Since my grandfather's license was revoked due to numerous DUI's, he relied on others to bring his liquor to him. Eventually my grandmother found out Bill Green was one of his so-called delivery persons. She was so angry, because she had tried so hard to keep him sober. But that was not to be.

There were times my grandmother would leave us alone with him. She loved to go to the Legion hall to play bingo and many times she'd win the jackpot, bring home a lot of money, probably $100 on those nights. Many times I'd be sitting next to him and watching tv. That is when he would slide his hand into my panties and touch me in my private areas. I never liked feeling his fingers inside of me. As Kathy remembers, I was his favorite.

Other times his friend Bill Green would stop by to bring him his bottle. My grandfather would pay him and then somehow Kathy and I would find ourselves sitting on their laps. My grandfather would have me and Kathy would sit on Bill's lap. This fondling and molestation would continue until we hit puberty.

Later in life, after my grandfather died, I'd hear that Bill Green had met his fate. His body was pulled out of the Mersey river where he drove off a bridge one snowy night and perished, drowning alone.

I can always remember how tense our house was. My grandmother never knew what she was coming home to. I'm sure she lived in fear dreading to open the door to another night of verbal, physical, and mental abuse. It was like a war zone. Everyone would take protective cover to avoid making my grandfather angry.

Kathy and I would retreat and watch, never knowing what would happen. I can still see my grandfather with a rifle sitting by the table and threatening to kill himself. My grandmother would eventually get hold of the gun once he got so drunk and passed out. But that would take a while, so for hours it seemed like the war went on and I was so scared he was going to kill her. He would move the gun and yell that he'd had enough, pointing the gun directly at her.

To him, his demons were real. He hated everyone when he was drunk. So I learned to step on eggshells, never provoking him, but to keep quiet and calm; although inside I was petrified. I know Kathy was too.

Reflection

There's a place I go where no one will know,
it's where no one can see or even reach me.
I close my eyes and it appears,
my safe place where there are no fears...
secluded and warm I can stop to be...
away from all fears and anxiety.
It washes over me;
the calmness can make me feel whole and able again...
to face another day with renewed strength that grows within.
I feel replenished, for I know, we all must have a bad day or two,
but regardless it will get better for you...
Don't get discouraged, just move ahead,
dark days, don't stay, but look carefully ahead,
for that opportunity to make a change in you,
be grateful and patient for what you do,
for there are others who will always rely on you.

Sometimes we would over-do trying to meet deadlines, keeping up with work, home and school activities ... it's important to analyze and prioritize what is necessary and let other things wait ... anxiety comes from pushing yourself too much. We must step back and look at the big picture ... and most of all realize that we are one person and we can only do what we are capable of, let some things go ... in the end you will be a more patient and giving person if you can reduce the stress.

My grandmother never knew, but when she was away, we were molested by our grandfather and his friend. It happened many times, we couldn't make much sense of it then, but grew to understand more when we hit puberty and learned it in school; by then it stopped but the damage was done ... a secret we kept until my grandfather died. Only then did I tell my grandmother.

Kathy and me pictured in 1969 in front of
our grandmother's rock garden.
I was 6, Kathy was 9

Reflection

I've been where many people will never go...
I've learned that life can be hard, so...
being forced to survive,
you will do what it takes to stay alive,
you will look for the light to shine in
and grasp that small ray, to begin...
to find hope in all small things,
to never give up on your dreams.
Hope that sustains you giving you that rope, to hang on,
to feel the sun that warms your face before the day is done...
to look and see the kindness to be
from those who emerged timelessly...

that nurture and feed your very soul,
to refinish and make you feel entirely hole.
I do not dwell there anymore,
for I found peace and forgiveness to stand once more.
That is where my memories go
and from where my wisdom grows.

My father holding Kathy, my mother pregnant with me

Chapter 6
Teen Years

Someone once told me that in childhood we form patterns. Those patterns turn into habits, and those habits become character.

As Kathy and I grew up, we made a few close friends at school, but most of the time that was the only time we would see them. We primarily had to play in our yard, there were no sleepovers or birthday parties or school functions we were allowed to attend. Looking back, I'm sure this was because my grandmother secretly wanted no one to know how bad our grandfather drank. If he was drinking or got drunk, his personality was unpredictable. So, we were very much isolated, much like my grandmother.

I can remember how hard I tried to fit in at school just wanting that acceptance. I exceled at running and basketball since I was very tall, being one of the tallest girls in the class. So one time my coach came to our house to ask if I could join the high school basketball team, but I was not permitted to by my grandmother. I was so let down, upset and angry.

At school, being a teenager came with a lot of bullying. I was teased for being tall and skinny, and chastised "Skinny Minnie" and "Bean Pole" or "Heather Feather what's the weather?" There were those girls that wanted to fight and pick on me. My sister always came to my rescue to fight my battles; fist fighting and all. I was always quiet, shy, and introverted.

It was difficult to fit in with the cool kids, because I had hand me down clothes and no new fashions. My jeans my grandmother bought me were always too big, so at night I'd sneak thread and a needle and sew them up in the seat so that I wouldn't be teased for baggy jeans. Then, I'd have to pull out the threads to put them in the wash, so she wouldn't notice it.

So the next time I wore them, I'd need to do it all over again. I just wanted to fit in.

I was teased for oily hair. We were only allowed to take one bath a week, as we had a shallow well and water was rationed to get us through the dry summer. I'd wait until everyone was sleeping and sneak downstairs to wash my hair in the sink. I had every step calculated so I wouldn't step on the creaky stair and wake anyone up. Once downstairs, I worked quickly to wet, wash, and dry my hair with a paper towel, counting the times I heard the water pump run. I knew that it was okay for it to run one or two times, like I was using the bathroom, but no more or my grandparents would wake up and discover what I was doing. I never was caught and continued this practice until I was eighteen and moved out.

It was so hard to face the other kids who always were dressed well and had their hair done, and girls with their makeup on. We were not allowed to wear makeup or paint our nails, and haircuts were done by my grandmother. Occasionally my aunt Cheryl cut our hair in her own beauty shop. That was a treat.

Reflection

Behind the smiles, laughter and tears,
there lurks a child beyond her years...
time and time again she could feel,
the pokes and hurt and sometimes for real...
it made her see that some things in life can't be...
to flee and look beyond despair,
among the piles of empty promises, she finds it there...
and life has shown her many things,
are not what they appear to be...
she struggles, fell but found herself, finally to be free...
to touch and see, feel and love is what is most valued...
your worth is not for someone else to control...
your presence is beautifully your own
and you can be anything you choose...
just believe so.

On the farm, sometimes animals were sick or born with defects, our grandfather would bring them inside in a box, until they recovered or got stronger. On occasion, a hen or duck would refuse to sit upon their nest, so he would bring in the eggs, set them in a box with a light, to keep the eggs warm. We had to turn them every day. Sure enough, eventually they would hatch, and we would find the cute fuzzy yellow or black chicks or ducklings in there. So precious. My grandfather could be so kind and caring when he wasn't drinking alcohol. One of my favorite pets was Chirpy. She was a baby chicken born in the wintertime in the barn. At birth she was different, and I got to keep her in the kitchen in a box, she wouldn't be able to go with the other hens or roosters, they would probably kill her. Her beak and feet grew, but her body didn't, she was very small. I had her that winter and into the spring and she passed sometime over the summer. I found her dead in her box one morning. That was a sad day for me.

There was one kitten I could never forget, I named him Tar Baby. He was all black, I adored him and couldn't wait to get home from school to see him. On this day, my grandfather was on a ladder on the side of the house. I don't remember if he was painting or fixing the window, however; he suddenly blacked out and fell off the ladder, as the ladder clattered to the ground, it struck Tar Baby on the head; he was playing beneath the ladder. I could just remember seeing his head on the ground, mouth bleeding and his body was jerking in the air up and off the ground convulsing. Our grandfather wasn't moving, just lying there still, we thought he was dead. Kathy called out for help, grabbed my hand, and we ran to Lucy's house, our closest neighbor.

By the time, we got back with our neighbor, my grandfather was leaning against one of the old cars, and the kitten was nowhere to be seen. We think he hid it somewhere. My grandfather had high blood pressure, so I'm not sure if that's the reason he fell, or if he had been drinking all day. Regardless, Lucy yelled at him for putting himself in his predicament when no one was home. I believe our grandmother was working or running errands.

For a long time after that, I had nightmares of that poor kitten suffering from such a horrible death. Just death in itself I had never seen, it was so sad and tragic to lose my beloved Tar Baby this way. My grandfather never spoke about that day. I'm sure he felt bad for causing the kitten's death.

Chapter 7
Trauma

To see, to remember, to comprehend. It all depends on where you are standing. If there was such a thing as a telescope that could be focused on the past, then I could say: look, that's us, let's find out what really happened.

So I organize, catalog, and number … I even dig up photos and poems that I've written so many years ago that I wonder who really wrote those, and I begin to doubt whether what I remember is true, or did something really happen, or whether I even existed.

Those awkward teenage years were understandably difficult. For me, at age 13 I grew tall over the summer and almost didn't know how to handle the growth spurt. I so wish my breasts had grown but only wore a small a cup. Hormones alone were raging, I had a crush on a few boys at school and it was fun to pass notes in class, but I didn't get to see them outside of school.

Kathy also had her share of boyfriends in high school that she liked to hang out with. Kathy at age 16, blossomed over the summer and had curvatures which I didn't, including a larger bra size. I was jealous of that, but I never told her.

When we first arrived in Canada, we always thought it was temporary and that once our parents resolved their issues, they would come back for us. Holidays were hard, no letters, no cards, no gifts, even on our birthdays. Our grandparents never spoke about our parents. Only when our Aunt Melita and Uncle Junior came home to visit from the states, did we here bits and pieces about Richard, our father. Nothing about our mother.

After their divorce, my father remarried and had a son named Christopher. He loved and adored him, as he had a buddy to teach mechanics to and to go hunting and fishing with him, which he loved to do. Incidentally, my father only came home once to see his parents 3 years after he moved out at age 23.

Summers were long, no school and more time on our hands. I got lost in my music listening to the radio and trying hard to write the words to the songs. Those words sung by The Carpenters, Bee Gee's, Supertramp, and many others I clung to. I found reading those words helped sooth me and gave me ways to cope with the pain I was feeling inside. I liked to pick berries and sell them at a stand that I'd put up at the end of our driveway. Cars would stop to buy blackberries, blueberries, and raspberries that I sold for $2 per quart. I was thrilled to make some spending money.

Kathy and I looked forward to" Privateer Days." It was held every year in our small town of Liverpool, Nova Scotia, complete with a parade and food vendors, games, and face painting. We could attend this. It was something we looked forward to; getting away from the routine of staying home and meeting and mingling with other kids our age.

It was on one evening, we were all at the dinner table, my grandfather had been drinking all day. As usual, he liked to pick on someone, and Kathy was chosen this time. I don't remember what provoked him, but suddenly he slammed down his fork and yelled at Kathy, "You are not one of us." Kathy suddenly burst into tears and fled from the dinner table. My grandmother followed.

I was shocked and sad at the same time. Kathy had always felt different and this loud outburst just made her feel so unloved and unwanted. She remembers my grandmother telling her why my grandfather had said, that. She explained that our father met and married our mother knowing she was pregnant and gave Kathy his name. Our grandfather never apologized for the outburst. For Kathy, she figured this was his way of telling her. Regardless, Kathy felt she already knew, deep down.

Kathy always felt different and was treated as such. We didn't resemble each other at all. Kathy had long, straight, almost black hair with almond shaped brown eyes. On the other hand, I had curly blonde hair with blue eyes and was very tall. One Saturday, my grandmother was off in town doing grocery shopping. Kathy and I were doing our chores, dusting, vacuuming and cleaning. My grandfather liked to do the crossword puzzles and routinely got the neighbor's paper once they were done with it. So he sent Kathy over to get the newspaper from our elderly neighbor who lived across the street.

Garneau Seamen was retired, and his wife was in the hospital dying of cancer. I write about this happening from my sisters' memoir as she remembers it. Kathy went to the door and knocked. Garneau answered wearing a robe and she followed him into the kitchen. All of a sudden he turned, pulled down her elastic pants and grabbed her, pushing her to the floor. In the next moments, she remembers him straddling her after he opened his robe and his naked body was there in her face. Kathy froze. She was in shock, frightened and scared.

She remembers him going through the motions, but his penis wasn't erect. Kathy just wanted to get away. Suddenly, he got up after hearing a noise outside and went to investigate. That's when Kathy started breathing again. Shaken, she jumped up, pulled her pants up and dashed out the front door. He called out after her, "Please don't tell anyone."

Kathy ran across the road and down our long driveway. Our grandfather was waiting, and he knew when she ran inside something was wrong. Kathy told him everything, he calmed her down he calmed her down and promised to tell our grandmother when she got home. Kathy was unsure of where I was when this all happened.

Eventually, our grandmother returned, and they went over to confront him, telling Kathy she had to go too. Kathy said no but had to and she stood behind them as Garneau Seamen opened the door. They confronted him with the allegations, but he denied it. Kathy was scared and crying, he told them to stay there, left and returned with a bible. He placed his hand on the bible and swore it never happened. That's when our grandparents knew he was lying, for Garneau never believed in religion, God or the bible. They believed Kathy. Some colorful words were exchanged by my grandfather, then they went home.

Shortly after the sexual assault, Garneau moved away. The sad thing about all of this was that his wife was an absolute sweetheart. Her name was Doris and we all loved her. She and my grandmother were very close at one point. She was a good person.

Two weeks later, another terrible thing happened to my sister. I will explain in her words from her memoir, as this memory still haunts her today. It was a Saturday and Kathy age 16 would babysit for Norman and Lisa who had three children. They lived up the road from us walking distance.

She walked over bringing her math homework with her and arrived at their house. Lisa explained to Kathy she was driving into Halifax to do some shopping, Norman was there working on a car in the garage as he was a mechanic, and the children were inside. Lisa told her to call upon Norman if she needed anything. Kathy said thanks and told Lisa to enjoy her day shopping and Lisa left.

Kathy turned her attention to the children and asked them if they wanted to play in the backyard that was fenced in. They all shouted, "Yes!" and Kathy explained to them to go out and she'd join them later after she finished her homework. The children agreed and out they went.

Kathy went to the living room to get out her homework, it was a sunny and warm day outside. She never heard Norman enter and lock the outside door, so the kids would not be able to come back inside. Then he came up behind her as she was sitting on the couch. Norman never uttered a word but startled her as he grabbed her and lifted her over the couch. Her books went flying, as he headed to the bedroom as if he had a mission to do.

Kathy was in total shock and ridged with fear. "What was happening, not this again!" It all came rushing back. But this time it was far worse. The mind is a powerful thing, it protects by dismissing unhappy or hurtful times. She had blocked out much of her past for years and never remembered. It took her a lot of counseling and talking for years to heal.

Norman continued, he had a mission and with no talking he ripped off her clothes and threw them on the floor. He had her by the arm, she couldn't run, she was crying and saying "no! no! no! no!" over and over again. He had his pants down around his ankles and sitting on the edge of the bed, he lifted her up to straddle him.

He tried to enter her forcing himself, he was rough and strong. It hurt bad, she froze but once the pain started, she cried out "No" and tried to get away struggling. Her cries fell on deaf ears with him, she could hear the children banging on the back door probably hearing the commotion inside.

Suddenly Norman heard something and stood up sending Kathy falling back onto the floor. He quickly pulled up his pants and dashed out, leaving her there sobbing and crying in pain. She scrambled to grab her clothes, crying and shaking, she noticed the blood running down her leg. Then she heard Lisa's voice as she walked into the bedroom.

Lisa stared at her as Kathy rushed to put on her clothes, sobbing and crying. Lisa Norman grabbed her as she was trying to pick up her strewn books from the living room floor. Lisa saw all of this. Kathy was so upset as she looked on, Lisa seemed so calm, it scared her. Lisa had returned home early because she had forgotten her list.

Kathy rushed out the door and ran all the way home. She felt sick, guilty, dirty, and nauseated. She was trembling like a leaf when she got home. I don't remember this. I'm not sure where I was, but our grandmother and grandfather were there. Kathy told them what had happened. Our grandmother took her to the doctor the next day. Dr. Large was the towns family doctor, he examined Kathy and explained to our grandmother that there was trauma injury and the hymen had been torn but not completely. There was sperm present and no pregnancy, she was still a virgin, but the bleeding would continue for the next 3 days. She had bruises and scratches on her body.

All of this was so traumatizing, and Kathy remembers the words of the doctor when our grandmother asked him a question. My grandmother asked, "Why do you think this happened to her?" Dr. Large answered, "Sometimes it's just the way the girl looks, her walk and it just happens." Those words resided in her head almost like she had asked for it and she was raped all over again, remembering that comment in later years. The injustice was crippling. For in the 1970s, in a small town there was no sexual assault or rape reported and no rape kit collected. It was almost like nothing had ever happened, just kicked under the carpet. In later years, Kathy would find out from an old high school friend who also revealed she had been raped by the same man when she was their babysitter.

Reflection

It was as if she wasn't there...
his hands violently grabbing her,
her voice gone, mouth open, nothing coming out...
frozen, almost like watching a movie from a screen,
she wanted to shout, she wanted to scream...
crushing her, his weight felt like a boulder...
taking forever, how still were the hands of the clock...
the pain wrenching inside of her,
tears running down from her face,

there was nowhere to run to,
there was nowhere safe...
and then as abruptly as it started,
it was done...
but the memory and flashback would haunt her forever...
in her nightmares it lived on.

I think of this day. I think of all the fear Kathy must have felt. I think of all of those who failed her and not believed her; our grandparents, the doctor who never took the assault seriously. I applaud her strength, her efforts to put her life together again to become a mother, a good-hearted person, a hard worker, a photographer, and a lover of peace. My sister was a rape survivor, she overcame a nightmare, and she shines like a star now. I will always look up to her, my protector, my big sister.

Kathy pictured with her 3-legged cat "Mama"

Chapter 8
The Separation

Top step Grandfather, Kathy, and I
with our Grandmother pictured with relatives visiting

After this happened, I had a lot of questions for Kathy, but I can't remember how she explained it. I just knew something horrible had happened and there was a lot of tension and anger in the house as I sensed my grandparents were stressed and upset.

On Monday we went to school as usual, as if nothing had happened. It was not talked about to us by our grandparents. Then, arriving home from school that day, we were met at the door by my grandmother. She allowed me in, but not Kathy. She told her "to go away and never come back!" As if Kathy was not hurting enough, she was being rejected by her own grandmother.

Kathy was shocked, hurt and crying as my grandmother shouted that she was a bad influence on me, and that she was doing these things to just get away. Kathy cried and said it wasn't her fault, she was good. My grandmother yelled that she was just like our mother, to "leave and never come back". Kathy could hear me crying on the other side of the door.

Kathy stood there in disbelief, upset, she hung there for a while. She only had her backpack, empty lunchbox, and the clothes on her back. Where should she go? What should she do? After a while, she decided to walk to her best friend's house, Tammie Hatt. Once she got there, Kathy told Tammie's mom what had happened. She gave her 20 cents (two dimes), to go use the payphone to call the police. She didn't want any trouble.

Kathy made the phone call and waited, scared and by herself. Before long, a car drove up and a mountain of a man got out. At first Kathy wanted to run, a flashback of Norman came to her, he was huge too. He saw that she was scared, he kept his distance and she realized he was a cop in uniform. His eyes were kind as he introduced himself as Gary Grant. He explained everything to her as he listened to her story and explained he would be driving her to the police station to take a report.

After taking down names and explaining everything to her, he said these words, "I believe you." That's how Kathy's healing began, a stranger believed her, whereas her own grandmother didn't. Then he told her, because of her age he really didn't want to put her in the system as she needed a place to live. Kathy knew those words as both her and I had been in and out of foster homes when we were younger. He explained he I'd like her to meet his wife, and they were offering to let her stay with them until a more permanent solution could be figured out.

Kathy stayed with these wonderful people for two weeks, until it was decided she'd live in Bridgewater with our Aunt Sally and Uncle Keith. Gary Grant arranged her permanent residence with them and picked up Kathy's clothes from my grandparents. He continued to keep tabs on Kathy for years and to this day they are still friends. Kathy considers him her guardian angel and is forever grateful for everything he did for her at this traumatic time in her life.

In the meantime, I had no contact with my sister. We had no phone and I didn't even know where she was. I was completely lost and missed her terribly. I became more introverted, shy, and found music and writing helped me cope with the sadness and loneliness. I could not ask about her, as this just angered my grandparents. I suffered in silence, crying myself to sleep many nights. School became worse, as I had no big sister to stand up for me with my bullies. I devised clever ways to get home after school, finding different routes and shortcuts to avoid them.

It became more chaotic at home as my grandfather would get drunk and take it out on me or my grandmother. He'd bring up the fact that my grandmother kicked Kathy out of the house, and he'd torment my grandmother repeatedly about that. His anger was like releasing the lions; he loved to badger her until she broke down crying.

I remember seeing her with her hands covering her face, trying to regain composure as she knew I could see and hear them arguing. Many times, I saw the bruises and scratches on her arm, and I knew how she had gotten them. Eventually I began to steal cigarettes from my grandfather and when my grandmother left the house to go grocery shopping or to bingo, I would smoke. I knew my grandfather wouldn't notice, he was too drunk to, so I'd go upstairs, open the window, and smoke. I was 15. It seemed to calm me and put me in a fog. It was as if I wasn't there for a while, but once the feeling wore off, the smoke cleared, and I knew where I was.

In school I met a friend who was the minister's daughter. Her name was Susan. Much like me, she was very shy and picked on at school. We had a lot in common as she was very sheltered and restricted, being her father was the minister of the church.

Before long, my grandmother allowed me to go to her house and eventually sleep over. I think my grandmother felt sorry for me as I no longer had my big sister and she trusted them since they were a church abiding family. Susan and I experimented with drinking, and the alcohol and cigarettes helped dull the pain inside of me.

We would hang out at the Milton bridge where a lot of the cool kids drove by and they could see us. It was nice to break free from my house and get away from the constant fighting that occurred on a daily basis. We were trying to fit in and be cool.

Then one day, I came home from school and as usual my grandfather was there. I could tell he'd been drinking all day and was already getting agitated. My grandmother wasn't home yet, and this also angered him, as he always wanted her there to fix him a cooked dinner.

I don't remember what I had said to him, but before I knew it I was lying on the floor and his hands were wrapped around my neck choking me. I still remember how cold and angry his eyes looked as I struggled to get away. Somehow, I got to my feet and fled; he didn't follow me. I didn't tell my grandmother when she got home. I knew it would only upset her.

The next day I had to go to school, and I could see the finger marks and bruises on my neck, so I wore a turtleneck sweater to cover them. My grand-father never said a thing to me, no apology given. It was as if it had never happened. He typically would not drink the next day after binging, so I think he had blacked out and really hadn't remembered the violent acts he did. He was such a miserable person when he chose alcohol.

Before long, I noticed a white van that always drove by us when Susan and I would be hanging out at the bridge. I came to find out his name was Doug and his younger brother Brent was the cool kid who had parties in his basement on the weekend with his parent's approval. All the girls found Brent hot, I never thought I'd be invited to one of his parties, as I wasn't considered one of the party girls. However, his oldest brother Doug liked me so that's how I became invited and accepted. Doug was four years older than me turning seventeen, it was exciting to have someone interested in me. I had never had a boyfriend, but I so wanted one.

Before long, I began to lie to my grandmother and tell her I was going to the store and over to Susan's house. I'd leave, and Doug would pick me up once I was out of sight from the house, and before long he introduced me to drugs. The vodka I drank relaxed me. I felt so calm with no worries and for a while I could forget all my troubles. He always had weed and rolled his own joints.

We drank and smoked cigarettes and pot and before long we'd be making out in his white van. He always knew a place to drive, where it was secluded. He was a rocker with all the great music, with Rolling Stones, Kiss, or Rush playing in the background. We kissed and touched each other just fooling around.

Then one day, I decided to cut school and hang out with Doug at his house. We had the entire day, his mother had left for work and his brother Brent was in school. That's when I lost my virginity. We had never gone all the way before, but this time we did. We drank some screwdrivers and we passed around a joint. I felt relaxed, clam and ready. It felt nice to get naked pressing our bodies together, as we excitedly explored each other. He was patient with me, I remember thinking how big he was and after he entered me there was a sharp pain and I felt something warm between my legs. He continued to make love to me and then his groan was loud as he climaxed. He rolled off of me and then I saw the blood.

He was gentle and helped me wash up, he had used a condom, so I felt relieved to know that. We held each other for a while, he knew it was my first time. Later we cleaned up the sheets not to leave any evidence once his mother returned home. I felt totally in love with him, he seemed to understand my home life and all my issues. It was nice to escape in this world of alcohol, pot, and music that filled my head. Once I came home, my grandmother was waiting. She would frisk me feeling my pockets for cigarettes, lighters or anything else. I'm sure she could smell the smoke on me. I remember her asking me, "Where have you been, you should've been home an hour ago?" I didn't care, I couldn't really hear her, I was in a world of my own high and drunk but no more pain for now.

Reflection

Change let me look inside myself to see me.
It was not anticipated, but it enabled me to be ...
who I am today ...
it never came easy on that unexpected day ...
to dig deep into my gut wrenching pain,
to paint the picture, to enable my dream ...
to free myself of this life of hell,
to journey the path, to see as well ...
to experience situations that taught me lessons,
to feel what it was like to be free,
to make mistakes,
to grow,
to know that everything would be ok,

to live life and stumble along the dark way...
I never knew how lonely it could be...
without you, my shield, my big sister to protect me...
but deep down I always knew,
I could make it my way,
and in the midst of the storm,
I would find the light and be reborn.

Chapter 9
Troubles

No matter what I did, I could not shake the feeling that I was hopelessly alone. That my sister was gone, and that I'd never see her again. I was devastated.

As sisters, we had never been apart since moving from Tampa, Florida at age 6 and 9 to live with our grandparents. This would be my turning point in my life. I learned ways to deal with this loss in good ways and bad. Abrupt change gave me insight to manage the chaos in my home with my alcoholic grandfather, to find the strength to cope and survive.

Writing this now at an oh so distant age, I can still feel the pain all these years later. I suppose that I was suffering from regular everyday teenage anger, but it felt like so much more back then.

The next few years were filled with uncertainty, insecurity and worry, as I began to realize graduation was just a year away.

Suddenly I was a seventeen-year-old, desperately wanting my independence, my freedom, my own life to live. I was tired of imprisonment, of the barricades that my grandparents kept me in. I began to think hard on my situation and the ways I could get out.

I realized that I needed to make a choice on where I was going once high school was completed. My options were limited as my grandparents had no college fund for me to further my education upon graduation. My grandparents began to talk about me enlisting in the army, as that would enable me to learn a trade and find a successful career. I remember when I heard my grandmother talking about me seeing a recruiter to get more information, I wasn't happy. That was the last thing I ever wanted, to be in another restricted, disciplined place being controlled.

Kathy and I had always spoke about maybe returning to the states once we graduated. We had always known we had dual citizenship and we could go back one day if we wanted to. In my mind I knew I had to reach out to my biological father to see if he'd help me get situated and start a new life there. I got my father's address from one of my relatives, but I waited to write him.

The truth, I still wasn't sure that my father even wanted me. That was my truth at the time. That I wanted to go home, but I wasn't sure there was a home to go home to.

In school, I managed to get good grades, but the subject I loved the most was writing. Mrs. Conrad was my teacher and she always complimented many of my essays and projects. Many times, I'd doodle on math homework in class thinking of subjects I wanted to write about. I wrote some poetry and prose, and the subjects came from what I was dealing with at the time in my life, unknown to my teacher.

The thing I dreaded the most in school was to do a presentation in front of the class. I'd be told the dates in advanced when I was presenting. As that day neared, I'd get so anxious that I would not sleep the night before.

When called upon to present, I can still remember that feeling; my heart would be racing, palms sweating, as the blood rushed to my face. My voice would become shaky, I could hear the chuckles and jeers as I struggled to continue. It was as if their malicious laughter was tearing me up, piece by piece and discarding me.

I felt like I was on display, their looks piercing and seeing right through me. It was as if their jeers were seeing me transparent, raw and real, seeing me for who I was. All that I hid inside; the anger, resentment, frustration, and sadness of my situation at home, they could see it all. I just wanted to melt or crawl away and hide, or just die. It was terrible.

I felt very alone, sad at times for I really missed my sister. I wondered how she was doing, if she had changed, if she was dating and all those things. I just wished I could see her again, talk to her, and see if she was finally happy.

At home, nothing was different. My grandfather continued to binge drink and take his anger out on my grandmother. I remember the time he grabbed her and she fell down the stairs. I wasn't sure if he had finally managed to hurt her so much that she would need to see a doctor. Secretly I feared for her life, I heard the threats and saw the gun pointed at her during many drunken stupors. I learned to stay back and to walk on eggshells whenever he was drunk.

I continued to go to school daily and never spoke of the abuse I witnessed on a regular basis. It almost became the norm, I only noticed it was not normal when I saw my best friend's family interact. Susan's parents were kind and respected each other. I never heard arguing or heard anger in their voices. It was a nice retreat when I stayed over. I never divulged the abuse we lived through. I knew I needed to stay quiet.

Church became an excuse to get out and be with my friend. It was far better than staying in my house and witnessing the horrific fights. It's funny, but Kathy and I were made to go to church, but my grandparents never did. When my grandmother left to play bingo, I was always nervous until she returned. My grandfather would accuse her of cheating with my Uncle Wallace and berate her over and over again. In 17 years, I had never seen them hold hands, kiss, or show any signs of affection.

While grandmother was gone, I would keep busy listening to my radio, finding solace in the words of the songs that reached my heart and gave me courage to hold on. I knew that things had to be better, they couldn't be any worse. I dreamed of my freedom, any chance to be myself and continue my writing, pouring my pain into words on paper.

Reflection:

"Why" written Nov. 1980

Why is there hurt?
Why is there pain?
Why is there present this nagging again?
Why is there worry?
Why is there fret?
Isn't it easier to try to forget?
Can't one block out the darkness and sorrow,
And just cheer up to face another tomorrow?
There's got to be happiness,
I know that for sure,
Cause what's the use of living,
If there's nothing to live for...

Reflection:

"Troubles" written Dec. 1980

Pen and paper, my old friend –
I'm here to write my thoughts again
Decisions plague to clog my mind –
And sanity, I seem to find –
In expressing words in a special way,
To help me pass this coming day.
My troubles; big as they might be –
Are much too large for only me –
To work them out, for each their own –
The utter loss to be alone…
In time they will no longer stand –
Bits of growing grains of sand.

Chapter 10

My First Love

I can remember many sleepless nights, tossing and turning, just wondering what was going on with Kathy. I'd cry into my pillow at night. I missed her face, her voice, and just her. I wondered if she missed me, and if she would ever be back in my life again.

Then one day while in geography class I heard my name called over the pa system to report to the office. It alarmed me, I couldn't think of why I was being paged, but I could feel my heart beating faster as I proceeded there. Just inside the doorway, I was shocked to see my sister standing there. I hardly recognized her. Her hair was long and colored with highlights, she had makeup on her face, nails polished, and was dressed nicely with a warm fur fringed winter coat on.

I just started to cry, I couldn't believe she was there. We cried, and she reassured me she was good, everything was much better living with Aunt Sally and Uncle Keith. She was working and had a boyfriend, I couldn't stop looking at her, I was still in disbelief she was in front of me. It had been almost three years since we saw or spoke to each other. That meeting was short, but I had a phone number I could reach her at. That was one of my best memories of junior year.

I walked home from the bus stop that day with a sense of relief knowing my sister was doing well and very happy with her life. It wasn't easy to keep quiet and not tell my grandparents, but I knew I couldn't and shouldn't as it would just cause more conflict. I slept better that night, the best I had in a long time.

I can remember the close times Doug and I experienced together. Doug was introverted, but not around me; we always enjoyed each other. Sometimes we'd just listen to music and cuddle. Doug was my first love, the very first man I ever trusted with my heart. It wasn't easy for me to trust any man as all of those in my life up to this point only led to hurt and disappointment.

Doug was my sweetheart; I made every attempt to see him when I could. He was my best friend, my lover and confidant. As I continued to finish my final year of school, I still hadn't told anyone of my plans to go back to America, if that was my plan at all. I still hadn't called or written my father, for fear that he wouldn't want me.

I was also starting to feel anxious about the whole idea, leaving Doug —could I actually do that? It would also be hard to leave Susan. We were best friends, we had each other. Susan was much like me, introverted, shy, and naïve. Being the minister's daughter came with a lot of restrictions and the need to conform and be attentive to her actions and reputation. Any bad behavior would be reflected on her entire family. Her mother and father preached the good word constantly and did not look highly on her smoking or drinking. Susan's anxiety was so much, she'd twirl her hair in a nervous manor when her parents were scolding her or making her listen to them. It was her mother who made her take piano lessons, as she played quite well. Her father was the disciplinary and wanted Susan to be an example for others to live a religious, self-fulfilling life and to restrain from the evils in the world; those evils being sex before marriage, consuming alcohol, and smoking.

My best friend Susan was upset when I told her I was planning to leave Nova Scotia. We were inseparable, but she was excited for me to finally break away and experience life on my own. She was the one I first got drunk with, drinking vodka one Friday night. I vividly remember when she took a photo of me looking pale and sick when I was hung over the next day.

Years later, I'd hear that Susan had been married, divorced and had one daughter. She battled depression and Trichotillomania Disorder for many years. I then understood more about this, I thought back and remembered Susan being self-conscious of her thin hair, in some areas there were even bald spots. In a manner to deal with her anxiety, she'd tear her hair out, which would lead to areas of baldness and thinning hair, which only made her more self-conscious in school when other kids would tease her. School can be a very cruel place, as bullying will always be there and would never go away.

Reflection:

"Worry" written Dec. 1981

I was one of those in school, who was always eager to just "get through"
And now I'm here with my very last year,
The time has flown by,
The future is near.
"what will I do?"
"where will I go?"
Can I move on out of this dark hole?
Money is the problem,
Have I got enough?
The problems are countless,
The going is rough
Oh, I'll just drift around,
Just for a spell
It can't be that bad,
I'll just go on till...
My money is gone,
The weather is cold,
The rent is high
Sure is hard to just "skim by"
Questions are many,
They clog up your mind
Forever bugging you,
Occupying your time;
To figure them out,
Line up your life
And just hope to God, that things will turn out all right.

As my graduation approached, I was full of apprehension for my future. I don't recall attending the prom and don't have a yearbook to review. I'm sure cost was the issue. Therefore, I will never have those memories to relive. I regret that. I vaguely remember attending a high school dance and the song that resonates in my mind is "Crimson and Clover by Tommy James and the Shondells" and slow dancing with my "secret crush," Wayne. That song is one that still moves my heart, innocent love in the making, just pure and uninhibited, so much like me. I so wanted to be free.

As I said my goodbyes to my sweetheart, Doug, my sister and my best friend Susan, and all that I have known, I looked forward to the "awakening;" a time I could finally be on my own. It was scary. I played the scene out over and over in my mind, meeting my father, my stepmother, and four-year-old step-brother, not knowing what was next. I prayed life had to be better than the life I had here. I was ready to close this door and open a new door to a new life.

Reflection:

Find the fighter in you,
dig deep,
find a way,
knock down the walls of yesterday...
Your armor has been built,
it's strong,
this is not where you belong,
pierce those memories,
bleed away...
Hear the music rage on,
giving you hope to hang on...
Radiate your soul and encourage you in a way,
you must sustain your strength,
remember that pain,
but let it motivate you to make change.
Go forward,
glance only when you need to...
To give you the edge,
to move you...
To better things,

forget it all...
Stand up,
stand strong,
to prevent the fall...
Believe it,
believe in you,
there's absolutely nothing you can't do...
Fight for it,
never give up...
No one can stop
you, only you can do that...
Believe in you.

I was eighteen, it was an age of uncertainty, self-discovery, and worry. I so wanted my independence and worked hard to get that; I finally decided I'd move to Florida once I graduated in 1981. Music became my escape. I'd spend hours listening to bands like April Wine, Fleetwood Mac, writing the words to their songs, it gave me peace inside and the will to hang on. I'd be leaving Canada, leaving my sister, my boyfriend, my friends, and my grandparents, and starting over. I missed her, my sister, but I knew this was my only chance to break away and start a new life. I was scared, I would be meeting my father again thirteen years later and reopening those wounds of abandonment and pain. I'd also be also looking for my mother to try to get answers, to fill in all those unanswered questions I had when we were removed from our negligent parents. I'd be opening a new door to a new life.

Reflection:

Stay young in your heart,
Keep that music playing,
Regardless of where you are on your personal journey...
Never stop hearing the music
It was there when you were young
It will bring you back there...
Its transcending
Never ending
LISTEN!

Chapter 11
Turmoil

I found freedom through writing. I realized how lost I had become through writing. It had taken me a long time and much struggle to finally contact my father. I finally realized that my earliest writing was sort of sad and lonely. I would write about things that I fully didn't understand. Even as a teenager, I could feel an incredible sadness, a need for emotion, and a sensation of being in my adolescent pain. Sometimes things were so bleak in my head that I even thought about ending it all, and just checking out of this world; anything to end the pain of these dark feelings. Yes, it was finally time to contact my father.

I was very unsure; should I see him again? What was he like? Was he still an alcoholic? Would he answer me if I wrote him? I felt so detached from him, the name "father" was strange to say and in no way did I feel it was the proper name for him. A father would have kept in contact with me. He had not seen, spoke or reached out to me or my sister for 12 years. In fact, neither parent had. No phone calls, no gifts, no cards, no letters, simply nothing. It was as if we did not exist.

Reflecting now, at age fifty-six I can remember that even as a child, I knew I was different. I'd try hard to comprehend what had happened, those chain of events that brought me and my sister to Nova Scotia, Canada to be in the care of our grandparents.

Every holiday, Christmas, thanksgiving, Easter, Mother's Day, Father's Day, there was an empty void of despair. I so wanted to feel that connection, that of belonging to my real family. Kathy and I tried hard to understand what had occurred, and what circumstances brought us to be removed from our biological parents.

Kathy and I pictured with our parents during the holidays

Our parents were both alcoholics. My father would go to work every day as a mechanic; once work was done, he'd head to the bar. Some nights he'd come home, other times not. As we got older Kathy and I shared our memories and we were able to put things together. Things started to make better sense.

While my dad worked, our mother would stay home, but being an alcoholic herself, she worried more about her next bottle than taking care of her two girls. Since she was incompetent, and unwilling to be a mother to me, my big sister took on the role. On days when there was little or no food, my sister would pick avocadoes from our tree and we'd eat those. She looked after me, even changing and bathing me when our mother was passed out on the couch.

The neglect of providing basic care for us began to show. We were both underweight, had pinworms, and sores on various parts of our body. Frequent drives home by the police became almost routine at 3:00 am in the morning. My sister and I had little or no supervision. Sometimes our mother would leave us in the locked car for hours while she visited her "male friends". Once she returned, she'd have money, but very little got spent on groceries, most was used at the liquor store.

Eventually, DCF (Department of Children and Family Services) became involved and not long after we were removed from our home and put in foster care until the courts could determine if our biological parents were suitable or not. One of my most vivid memories was on my 5th birthday when my parents came to visit and brought me a gift while in foster care, it was an easy-bake-oven, something I'd always wanted. I was so excited when I opened the box. Kathy and I played with it while our parents visited, but we were not allowed to bake the cookies as our foster parents didn't allow it. This made me very sad and upset.

Kathy and I would be put in a few foster homes until finally the courts determined it was in our best interest that we would be removed from our biological parents due to ongoing neglect and abuse. As I think back, I can absorb the vicious cycle of how alcohol abuse and addiction influenced every aspect of my life. Once again I thought about how patterns become habit, and habit becomes character.

My mind drifts to my grandfather and I wonder what hell he went through as a child being one of twelve children. What unimaginable horror or abuse did he survive? My grandmother often mentioned when they were in an argument that his own father was a monster, a drunk who beat his wife Freda, but somehow, she survived years of abuse at his hands.

All that anger, suppressed guilt, shame and rage taken out on me, Kathy and my grandmother. I'm sure it was a learned behavior for my grandfather. His soul was tormented by his past childhood and the vicious cycle continued.

Today being an RN for 28 years now, I've treated many kinds of patients and I've seen the many effects alcohol has on the mind and body. I've seen alcohol encephalopathy with memory loss, mental conditions, bipolar, and cirrhosis of the liver from alcoholism. My own mother would be someone who suffered from alcohol encephalopathy and failure to thrive, its where the body wastes away with a thiamine or B6 deficiency which is prominently seen in alcoholics. They drink more alcohol and eat very little food. I would see this in my mother once I returned to Florida and years later it would contribute to her death.

So as I struggled at age 18 to decide my future, I was torn with a decision I had to make. I reached out to my Aunt Helen and Uncle Wallace as they stayed in contact with Richard, my dad. When Kathy and I visited them, they shared news about him. We knew he had divorced our mother and remarried and had a son, Christopher. From her letters, he had gotten his life together, no longer drinking and was working full time as a mechanic.

As far as my mother went, he mentioned she was living with her sister and husband in their house somewhere in Tampa. My mom's name was Robbie Campbell and she came from Tennessee. I wondered about her and planned to look her up once I got back to Florida.

I knew my future in Canada was bleak, no opportunity for college, no extra income to buy me a car. I was ready to move out and take my chances on reaching out to my father. It was unpredictable what would transpire in my house with my alcoholic grandfather, but I was willing to take the next step and write to my father.

I remember that my father had moved to Tampa Florida at age 18 and he only came home once at age 23 years I can only assume there was a falling out and again, I wondered if he also suffered greatly as a result of his own alcoholic father. In our house, Richard "our father" was never spoken of or mentioned. It was as if he had been written off and discarded. To think, he never came home again to see his mother or father, I wander what secrets lie there? I can only think he was tortured also, turning to the poison himself when he became a parent, drowning his pain in alcohol; as the disease continued to repeat itself.

I spent many hours writing the letter to my dad, writing, ripping it up, writing, ripping it up again. It was so strange to put my words on paper to a man I hardly knew; being apart for twelve years, having not heard his voice or seen his face, I felt detached and understandably so.

Anxiously, I awaited a response; I had post marked it with my aunt's address, so I eagerly awaited to hear from my Aunt Helen and Uncle Wallace. A few weeks later, they came by and brought me over for a visit and told me they received a letter from my dad. I read it word for word and excitely told them my dad had agreed to help me get situated. My ticket would be bought and sent to me; I was welcomed to return to Tampa Florida to start a new life.

Reflection

I've been where many people will never go…
I've learned that life can be hard, so…
being forced to survive,
you will do what it takes to stay alive,
you will look for the light to shine in
and grasp that small ray, to begin…
to find hope in all small things,
to never give up on your dreams.
Hope that sustains you giving you that rope, to hang on,
to feel the sun that warms your face before the day is done…
to look and see the kindness to be
from those who emerge timelessly…
that nurture and feed your very soul,
to replenish and make you feel entirely whole.
I do not dwell there anymore,
for I've found peace and forgiveness to stand once more.
That is where my memories go
and from there is where my wisdom grows.

I remember this house, this is where my sister and I grew up in Nova Scotia, Canada. I would spend 12 years there before moving back to Tampa, Florida. Within those walls of our home, there were turbulent times, molestation, incest, and abuse, my sister and I endured, and we watched our grandmother suffer abuse at the hands of our alcoholic grand-father. It was like living in hell at times when the yelling, arguing and violent attacks would occur. Kathy and I felt helpless to watch, and it was difficult to endure. We had each other, and we kept these secrets buried inside ourselves for years. Eventually my grandfather passed, and the house was torn down and the property sold.

Chapter 12
The Return

The day arrived, one that I had anticipated for a long time; one that I thought would never come. As I write this now, I try to remember all the details, I can not. It seems to come in bits and pieces. I don't remember the drive to the airport or the flight, but I do remember landing at Tampa International Airport. I had one suitcase as I exited the plane and followed behind the other passengers to the terminal.

I remember seeing them waving and as I looked up I could see them standing by the baggage area. I recognized my father, he looked much like a younger picture I had seen of him, but he was older and heavier. My little half-brother was smiling and wiggling and ready to leave as my stepmother continued to clutch his hand. My father introduced her to me as Pam, and I met Christopher for the first time. Pam had dark black hair; her skin was a golden brown. I would find out later that she was Cherokee Indian in nationality. My father led the way out and we all followed him to the car, it was evening 9 or 10 at night, humid and warm outside. We got into the car and left to head home, there was no AC in the car, so we had our windows down as we headed to the house.

As I sat in the backseat, my father spoke the most, he was proud to be driving the car we were in, that being a Pontiac GTO. He explained how hard it was to get the engine parts to repair and get the car in great working condition, but it was worth the hard work, this being his pride and joy. My dad was a mechanic by trade. He loved old cars, collected them, repaired them, and sold them for a living.

The drive seemed long, but after an hour or so we continued on Orient Road and turned onto Faulkenburg Road. At the end of the street, we turned into a gravel driveway. I could see the lights on in the house as we got out and approached the front door. It was a small house, much like Canada, but had no upstairs.

I was shown to my room and noticed it had a door. Unlike Canada, I had my own bedroom and privacy. It was small, I had a twin sized bed and a small dresser and closet. My bedroom was next to Dad and Pam's room. I later found out I had been given Christopher's room and he had been moved to their bedroom with a small bed in the corner. That night, I unpacked very little and made it to my bed to sleep, I was so tired.

I awoke the next morning when I heard scuffing sounds on the cement floor and realized Pam was up and fixing breakfast in the kitchen. Everyone got up and sat at the kitchen counter. Pam was busy frying eggs and bacon with toast for breakfast. It was the weekend, so dad was home too.

Before long, I made it outside and just like my grandfather, there were cars everywhere in the yard. Some were missing hoods, doors, trunks, and they were used to sell to collectors who needed parts and paid handsomely for them. Other cars were intact and in various stages of repair. It was a Mopars antique heaven to see some of these cars, legacies in their own lifetime. There were Roadrunners, Superbees, Coronets, Chargers, and a GTO.

Among the Mopars, my Dad was working on my car, a green 1973 Dodge Charger, with a 440-Hemi Engine that had dual exhaust. It looked like a green tanked monster. He explained that we would practice driving, as soon as I got my driver's license. I was very excited, but it would take time to learn.

I remember we drove to the DMV to obtain a book to study. I'd take my time to learn the book and in due time I'd practice driving. I was so excited to be able to finally feel like things were happening for me.

Then one day Pam told me her daughter Donna would be coming over to visit. I looked forward to that, having my 4-year-old half-brother around wasn't much fun. He was just a child; I grew bored quickly with his games. Donna was in her 20s and was driving, Pam told me. Finally, a girl I could hang out with, I thought.

That night I was restless and I got up to walk to the kitchen thinking maybe if I ate a snack I'd sleep better. I was shocked when I turned on the light. I saw black bugs crawling on the walls, the counter tops and scurrying to get away. One flew past me; large, ugly, and black. I quickly turned off the light, my appetite was gone after seeing that.

The next morning, I finally understood why Pam ritually got up early to clean and wipe the countertops, stove, and surfaces with Clorox bleach. She told me what the bugs were I had seen and to this day I can't stand cockroaches. I also later found out there were ways to use insecticides to control the infestations. My dad's house was simple, no ac, only ceiling and box fans. I'm sure that was another reason there were so many bugs. After this discovery I lost my appetite, ate very little; I couldn't erase the image, the roaches grossed me out.

That afternoon Donna came over and I was enthralled with her look. She was in her twenties, straight dark shoulder length hair, dark eyes, and her body was curvy with large breasts. She looked sophisticated with her eye makeup and brows done wearing bright red lipstick. I felt very plain next to her. My clothes were very simple and certainly didn't compliment my figure.

Before long, we planned a shopping day; she knew where all the discount clothing stores were, which sold brand names like Tommy Hilfiger, Ralph Lauren, and Nordstrom. It was surprising to see how small I really was, at 5'9" I weighed 120 lbs., tall and thin, and had somewhat of a figure with form fitting clothes on. Donna was fun, almost like my big sister. She took me under her wing, and it was nice to spend time with her doing girly things.

Donna was a beauty with her high cheek bones, much like her mother, the Cherokee Indian was her attribute. I soon found out that she spent a lot of time applying her makeup and would hear her arguing with her mom when she'd ask if she could borrow money to buy more. Her temper was quick, but so was Pam's. Pam was the ruler of the house; it was her word over my dad's and essentially, she managed his paycheck when he got paid.

Alcohol was never in the house and I learned that Pam was the reason for that. My father had stopped drinking, so occasionally if Donna brought alcohol over, and she offered my dad a beer, Pam would visibly get upset. I fully understood why. His personality would change quickly, he'd become a different person and a perfect of example of how pattern becomes habit, and how habit becomes character.

I remember him taking me to the drag races, he and a male friend drove us out to the racetrack. My dad was nice introducing me to his buddy, but once out of sight from Pam, he'd drink. Both would get louder and louder with each beer they consumed. My dad would start to flirt with me; grabbing my hand and looking at me in a different way. It made me feel uneasy; I was relieved to get back home when the races were over.

Once we walked in the door, I headed to my room and I could hear the arguing and accusations as Pam instantly knew he had been drinking once she had spoken to him. I began to feel like I was the cause and I tried to stay out of the way.

Then one day while I was in our yard, I met a young man who lived across from our house in a trailer park. David was his name; he was working on his car in his yard and he walked over to ask my dad for his advice on a repair. I instantly felt an attraction to him; he had blonde hair, a muscular build that I could see as he had no shirt on, just wearing his blue jeans. After he left, I couldn't stop thinking about him and that night, I noticed his window open facing our house and saw him moving about. I hoped he didn't have a girlfriend and I'd see him again soon.

Over the next few weeks, I practiced driving with my dad and Donna and soon after that I went to the DMV to get my license. I passed on my first try. I was so excited and proud of myself. Donna wanted to celebrate and so we planned a night out. We wore our hottest jeans; tight tank tops and our makeup and hair were perfect. She drove and we arrived at the nightclub before the band started.

I soon learned that guys flocked to Donna. She charmed them all and they were happy to buy her drinks, which she shared with me. We would be tipsy when we left the bar; at times I had to persuade her it was time to go. Donna was a party girl and I was the new girl from a small town. I noticed I drew a lot more attention from guys than I had in Canada. They'd all give me a second glance, smile and compliment me; remarks I hadn't heard in a long time. I loved the new me wearing trendy clothes and makeup. I felt pretty for once.

Reflection

Do I look in the mirror and truly see...
an image I'm happy with, that image who's me?
The world can be a cruel place to live...
It can take every ounce of breath I give...
it can chew me up and spit me out...
it can mix things around and plant the doubt...
it can be unforgiving, sucking the life out of living...
it can make me feel insignificant, almost nonexistent and small...
but I don't give into that...
for this is actually my call...
shake it off, find meaning for me, my passion,
my life is calling to—bring me to that "better place"...
don't lose my way now, but move with haste...
there's a lesson to learn here...
look in the mirror at my face.

Chapter 13
The Adjustment

Over the next few months, I was able to get my credentials in order. I applied for a Social Security card, showed proof of citizenship with my birth certificate and had my driver's license. I knew soon I'd need to get a job. I was looking forward to making my own money and spending it the way I pleased.

Pam took me to the health care clinic where I saw a dentist and over the next few weeks had dental care done. I had fillings replaced and saw a regular physician who gave me a wellness checkup. Once I answered the necessary questions, he also gave me a prescription for birth control pills. It was as if everything was happening so fast, but I was excited to be accepted as a young adolescent woman. I would never had been able to talk my grandmother into allowing me to receive contraception. No way!

I missed Susan, my boyfriend Doug, and my grandmother. I thought of them especially at night when I laid in my bed. I wrote and told them of all my recent accomplishments, receiving post cards in return. Then one day, I received a letter from Doug expressing how much he missed me and that he was planning to drive down and would arrive next month. He explained that once he had specific dates planned out, he'd inform me of them. I was surprised and was looking forward to seeing him again.

However, I felt torn in my feelings towards him, as I was enjoying my independence as a single woman free to do as I pleased. Donna and I were always going out and I loved all the admiration, flirting, and attention I received from other men. It was flattering and fun to flirt back. I even felt guilty about finding David so attractive, I wasn't sure where my feelings were.

During the week, I kept busy helping Pam clean the house and do laundry. She had an endless list of chores to do every day, so I tried to help her out. Donna, would come over, but she never really liked chores much. However, she did help with Christopher once he started kindergarten with his homework and coloring assessments. On the weekends, my dad would meet potential buyers who would come over to get specific car parts from the numerous Mopar cars he sold scrap parts from. The money he received from that he would purchase specific parts he needed to restore his antiques in order to get them back on the road in good driving condition.

It was hard work repairing and restoring these cars and many of them he sold to help pay the bills. He had the typical grease monkey hands with oil that was always difficult to scrub away from underneath his nails. I can still smell the special soap or degreaser he used to scrub with a brush under his nails and hands to try to lift the dirt away. Pam would constantly tell him to wash better before sitting down for dinner.

Finances were tight, they would argue over the bills and Pam would badger my dad to work harder to complete a car, so he could sell it and get paid. Sometimes my dad would finish a car and then he wanted to keep it, like his Pontiac GTO, but Pam would get very upset. Eventually, my dad got his way and managed to work extra hours at his daytime mechanic job to make ends meet. It was a constant juggle to manage the monthly bills with the ongoing repair and sales of the cars. Pam stayed home and managed the house meals and home repairs. She was a hard worker, like my grandmother; always busy.

One Friday night, Donna and I headed out, we had just enough cash to put gas in her car, but nothing more. We ended up at the club and before long the guys were buying us drinks. As it got later, the bar was closing so the guys suggested driving us to the beach. By this time, Donna was hanging onto one of the guys and the other one was interested in me. We were both very drunk and we couldn't drive. I don't remember the drive there, one of the guys drove. It wasn't so long until we arrived there. Before I knew it, I found myself making out with this guy, and I remember thinking, "he won't want sex for I'm on my period." That's funny when I think about it now. But it didn't stop him, and we had intercourse right there on the beach. It was wild, it was crazy.

As I laid there afterwards and over the next hour, I sobered up enough to realize I was out there alone, and I had no idea where I was or how I was going to get home. Everything was racing in my head; I was scared, then common sense took over and I convinced the guy to let me use his phone to call my dad to come and get me. Donna was nowhere to be found. Later I found out that she had left me there and went to her guy's place nearby.

I waited and waited, it seemed like forever, but my dad had to drive to Madera beach to get me, at least an hour drive away. By the time he arrived, the guy was no longer around and there I sat alone. My dad was angry, cursing as he helped me get into the car. I remember wiping the vomit away from my face with my hand before I passed out in the backseat during the long drive home.

In the morning, I found out that Donna had been driven back to the club and picked up her car in the AM. My father was angry at her and myself for putting him in this predicament. I felt terrible inside and I knew he was right. I also realized that Donna was not an angel and in no way did she care to be one. For Donna, life was all about the next party.

Although I had followed along, it was myself who made that decision to be there. It was then and there that I realized it was my own choice that put me in a dangerous situation. I suddenly felt my innocence wouldn't and couldn't protect me anymore. It was up to me to make better decisions the next time.

As I think back on this time in my life more than thirty-seven years ago, I feel fortunate to be alive. Anything could have happened to me; I was intoxicated and possibly drugged when I recall that night. I didn't even know this guy. I know now how easily things could have escalated and turned out badly for me. Inside I vowed never to put myself in a compromising position ever again. It was a real eye-opener.

Then one hot summer day, I received a post card from Doug announcing that he'd be here by the end of the week. He was making the long 2,000-mile trip driving his rusty old van from Nova Scotia, Canada to Tampa to see me. My dad and Pam agreed to give him their phone number to call us as he got closer to our home to give him better instructions to find us.

I was excited and nervous at the same time. It had been 7 months since I had seen or spoken to him. A few days before he arrived, I found out David who lived in the trailer park across from us was moving. I saw the truck backed in and saw him and his mother carrying boxes to the truck bed. I felt sad as I never did get to know him or hung out with him as I hoped we could have done. But again, I was 19 and he was in his late 20's. Maybe I was just a little girl to him.

The night before Doug arrived, he called and my dad gave him specific directions to find our house. I felt anxious as I waited for him to get there, we'd be together again soon, but I wasn't sure where that would find us.

We heard his van pull in; it was getting dark when he got there. We hugged and for those few moments it was like old times; I felt safe and secure. We all gathered in the kitchen and my dad, Pam, and Chris met him. He was still shy, and he spoke in short sentences not engaging them much. My dad asked him questions, he answered abruptly and before long they turned in for the night.

I gathered from our conversation that he had made the long trip to find out where we stood. I felt different around him; on one hand happy to see him, but on the other confused and not sure if I wanted to be tied down. He could tell I was being distant and different, not the quite shy girl I used to be. I was finding me; that had been hiding in big clothes with no make-up when I lived in Canada. It was as if I had come alive and now trying to catch up on all that I had missed. When I looked in the mirror now, I no longer saw the little girl that embarrassed easily, was insecure, and shy with no voice. Now my face was made up, my eyes bright with color with long black eyelashes, and lips that were pink with clothes that were flattering to my body. I finally felt pretty.

Doug and I took a drive in his van that morning. We caught up talking about our friends and things going on back in Canada. We made out; it felt awkward and I didn't feel that excitement like I used too. Doug stayed on for a few days and then he informed me that he had to head back, or his job would not be there for him.

Our last night together was a busy one, as my father had to work on his van motor for him to make the long trip back home to Canada. In my heart, and in my words, I said my final goodbyes to him as he headed back home. There were tears, but not in sadness, but in a sense, a release, a knowing that I was growing up, and I was strong enough to stand alone. I was experiencing life and making my own decisions, accepting the good and the bad, but learning life lessons along the way.

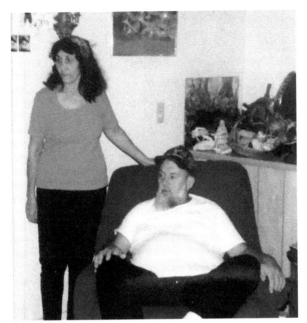

Richard and my step mother

Reflection

It wasn't by chance,
I came to be
...
It took choices and sacrifice,
To find the best version of me
...
I fought, I tried
Sometimes I died
...
Inside
Over and over again,
But I never gave up
...
I tried
Again and again
Always believing,
There was a way
...

To find the road
To break away
...
No refuge,
No free pass,
No re-entry
Did I see
...
Only difficult roads
Dim lights
And darkness for me
...
But perseverance,
Faith,
A will to go on
...
I traveled to see
And on my journey
There were low points along the way,
But it was those mistakes that built me up
To be my self today
...
I don't regret life's lessons
They were harsh and cruel
But my heart was young
and my decisions reckless like a fool
...
Now many tears and years later I know
There's a sparkle in my eyes
A smile and a glow
For all that I am today is pure
...
And I know from experience
That life can be unsure
But I have all I need inside
I can be

For I have found the best version of me.

Chapter 14
Further Abuse

Suddenly, as I write this, I feel unnerved by how much I have forgotten. I have some photographs, some scattered scraps of paper, some poems that I've written, but I can't say why I kept precisely those scraps rather than others, what I wrote, and why.

I think I remember what happened, but I'm really not sure of the why. I believe it was around this time in my life that I realized that I was running. Running harder and faster than was possible. But from what?

One night my father came into my bedroom and said, "Shhh be quiet, Pam won't know I'm here. She'll think I got up to eat something from the fridge." He slipped in my bed. I could feel him pressing his penis against me, my mind was racing. I told him to stop and as he pressed my body close to him, I felt him cum against my silk panties, without penetrating me. I rushed out of my bedroom and ran into the bathroom. I waited and listened, I was shaking and upset. He was gone when I went back to bed. It was that moment when I knew I had to go, just get away as quickly as I could. I felt dirty, unclean and used.

It was at age 20, I started running, trying hard to get away from all the mess, the devastating consequences of dealing with 3 generations of alcoholics. It would be a long painful process to get there though.

I ran to the next man; Saul was a good guy and I had met him through Donna. I was twenty and he was five years older. We were in love and we pretended that our pets were our children. We had a cat, and a dog named Shadow. We didn't have a lot of money, but we made the best of things, eating hot dogs, ramen noodles, and bologna many nights for dinner. Saul was not a big drinker; he only had a few beers from time to time, but he liked smoking pot more. Only after the honeymoon ended did we resort to swinging to spice things up and stay together. That was the end for us. It broke us completely and we drifted apart and went our separate ways; we were together for three years. Today, thirty years later, we are still friends. We laugh about how life was "easy" and despite having little money we were so happy.

Now as I look back, I realize how little I thought of myself. Being a child of an alcoholic, molestation, the grooming left me susceptible to engaging in promiscuity and, in fact, it had stripped me of my own self-worth and value. Something that I had learned as a child, seeing my mother engaging in adultery and prostitution.

I know for a long time that I was in denial, as I continued this reckless path of finding "broken people." It was easy for me to try to "fix" someone else so that I wouldn't look at helping myself. Then I met Joe, who was a barback. He drank a lot and avidly used cocaine. I engaged also; the drinking was out of control. He had a bad temper when he got drunk. I saw him put his fist through a door whenever he was angry with me or someone else, but he never touched me. Thinking back, I mistook abuse as love for that was how I was conditioned to think. When I arrived home from work one night, I caught Joe beating my small yoriki dog Shadow. Again, I took off running.

As I looked for direction and purpose, I eventually found it when Robert came into my life. I was twenty-three and a hostess at a Mexican restaurant. I remember the day he walked in; opening the door and tapping his white cane as he made his way up to the hostess stand. His hair was platinum blonde and he wore shades and spoke clearly as he requested a table for one. I took him to a table explaining there was one step he needed to make to sit there. He was engaging, asking me what the specials were and such. From that day on, he became a regular and showed up only when he knew I was working. I found that out later from a waitress friend of mine.

Robert and I were together for four years. I learned that he was twenty-three and in the army when the accident occurred. He was out on leave on a Saturday night with his date and best friend, who had arranged the blind date. After a night of partying, they headed back to the base. His best friend was driving when he went off the road and struck a tree. His best friend died; the others were lying in the dirt when the paramedics arrived. Robert was conscious when the paramedics began to triage.

Suddenly Robert became hemorrhaging and blood poured out of every orifice. He was trached and rushed to the hospital. Upon awakening days later in the ICU, he found out that he was completely blind from losing too much blood from the optic nerve. Since he was alert and oriented, the nurses had to ask him permission to amputate his right leg below the knee. His leg had been broken and became gangrenous in the cast after a week recovering. That was the hardest thing he had to do, to give them permission to do the surgery and to lose his leg to save his life.

I never knew Robert before his accident, but over the next few years it was he who guided me into my profession today as a RN. There was nothing he wouldn't do, he waterskied, he worked out at the gym, and attended HCC to obtain his pre requisitions in education in order to get his master's in teaching. Anyone who met him loved him. He was that kind of person.

Since his accident had occurred on the army base, he received full medical benefits and there were no financial worries for us. He bought me a '65 Mustang Fastback and an '84 Mustang Convertible GT 5 Speed. It was Robert who taught me how to drive a stick shift. We practiced in a grocery store parking lot; he shifted, and I drove until I learned how to shift drive on my own.

One of the surprising memories I have is when Robert asked me if he could drive his car for the very first time. We were in south Tampa leaving McDinton's bar and grille and he talked me into letting him drive just a few blocks down the road. He still had a valid driver's license that he had renewed prior to his accident. I was sitting in the passenger's side and steering as he controlled the gas, the brake and the shifting.

As the light was turning red, I told him to slow down; instead he abruptly braked short. Then I saw the police lights behind us pulling us over. Robert handed him his driver's license, registration, and proof of insurance; and as the policeman continued, Robert got out and stood by his car. Then after a few questions, he allowed Robert to return to the passenger's seat and I drove us the rest of the way home.

One week later as Robert was working out at the gym, he started telling his friend about our adventure; laughing and saying how cool it was for him to drive his new mustang for the first time. As he was explaining the story, a voice piped in from behind "Wasn't that Platt Street where you were pulled over?" Robert grew quiet and that's when he found out that the cop who had pulled him over knew him from the gym, knew he was totally blind and an amputee. Unbelievable. That's how Robert was; an inspiration to all who knew him.

I learned a lot from him; patience, empathy, compassion, and self-reliance. On his dark days, he'd be very quiet, and he'd slip into that mood. I knew to leave him alone; that he would work through it. Other times, he'd suffer phantom pain, grimacing and holding tight on his amputated limb describing it as a "knife cutting into his leg and foot" that was no longer there. As a nurse, I'd learn that phantom pain resulted from the severed nerves that ran to the limbs and although the limb is now gone the patient can feel pain as if the leg and foot is still there.

I loved him and we had four years together; we were engaged to be married, but I grew impatient not knowing if he'd commit or if we'd ever set a wedding date. At twenty-seven, I felt my biological clock was ticking and that it was time to settle down, get married, and begin a family. Robert continued his education and went to Michigan to complete his master's in teaching. I was a medical assistant and worked for an ENT doctor/ plastic surgeon. Time went by and we drifted apart, as he had made new friends and gained interest in his classes in Michigan.

Over the next six months we decided it was best to move on; we cried and we both knew it was for the best, our interests were not in the same place. Marriage was not something he wanted to jump into, he was more focused on his education. I felt it was more my idea than his to get married, so we broke up. I continued to stay on in the town house and take care of things until he could return.

Over time, I met my soon to be husband. We were both young, twenty-seven and full of life. We were married twenty-three years and had two beautiful boys that I'm so thankful to have. After our youngest was born, he celebrated five years of sobriety. However, relapsed again and told my oldest son who was eleven at the time, "I'm going to start drinking again, but don't tell your mom." Ultimately, his alcoholism would lead to our divorce. I suddenly realized how much this addiction had cost me.

Now here at age fifty-six it's been three years since I've been divorced. I've had considerable time to reflect, grow, and finally take a good look at myself. I've been able to analyze, look back from all I've been through as a child into the present and recognize why some things happened and ways I could better myself. I had to learn to love myself again. It would be a difficult process, but I was finally ready to stop this damn running.

I was beginning to make sense of all those failed relationships and why I kept repeating the process. It was as if the clock was ticking, but the second hand stood still. It was time to make lifetime changes. It was time to look at breaking echoes, all those repetitive "enabling" relationships that had stolen my life and made me the prisoner. I was ready to look in the mirror and work on me.

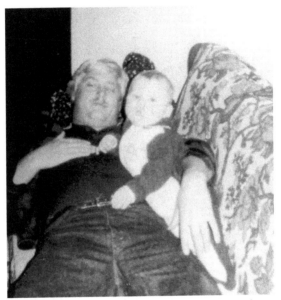

Robert pictured with Ryan on a visit to Canada

Reflection

I'm not the same person I was before
...
I've taken the chiseled pieces to adhere them back together
...
For they were broken,
Sharp,
And jagged
...
Pieces that pierced my heart
And like a broken mirror
I've put them back together
...
To build a new fresh start
Each piece took something from me
I wasn't sure how to heal
It took me years to recover
A lifetime
I needed to bleed and feel
...
To let go of the anger,
Resentment,
In order to thrive
Not to dwell in self-pity,
Or run,
Or hide,
...
But to bloom and grow,
For now, I know,
Life is what I make it to be,
I am alive and finally free,
To be myself,
...
To be me.

Reflection
Change
Change is evolving,
Its inevitable...
Sometimes forced,
It broke you with death,
Separation or divorce...
Change,
Its uplifting,
From teens
To
Adults
It brings,
Opportunity to experience something new,
To forget the fear and work on you...
Change is freedom,
To choose in middle years
And beyond
...
We are aging and dying
Learning and adapting,
Putting forth effort in order to see
...
That change is not to be
Ceased,
Feared,
Avoided,
Or forgotten
...
Take the time now to look in the mirror
And admire the face you see
...
For it was CHANGE that created you and will forever be,
A timeless entity.

Chapter 15
Kathy

My sister and I sprang from three generations of alcoholics. I am just beginning to realize that as a fact. I take all my thoughts, snapshots, poems, lay out all the pieces next to each other, lay them on top of each other, letting them bump against each other, trying to find a direction. For my sister Kathy, her journey has been different from mine. She has had more difficulty in attaining intimacy and maintaining long-term relationships due to the traumatic events she underwent as a child, that being molestation and rape.

Our grandmother's words "Go away and never come back" hurt enough. But to be told she was "Just like our mother" broke her spirit and self-worth. She would begin her healing once she moved to Bridgewater to live with Aunt Sally and Uncle Keith. As I read and reread her memoir, her words were, "I blossomed in Bridgewater."

Aunt Sally and Uncle Keith offered her independence and choices and above all they believed her story of what had happened when she was raped. She finally received counseling and kept psychologist appointments and began the healing process.

The first boyfriend she dated was Jeff, but soon she saw a different person when he started drinking alcohol. He'd be controlling, possessive, and angry. Uncle Keith, also being an alcoholic liked Jeff and drinking beers together they were oblivious to how this was harming her. In fact, Kathy didn't drink alcohol, quite the opposite of myself. She remembered all the bad stuff associated with it. Today she is only a social drinker; having one or two drinks and then stopping; not liking the feeling of becoming drunk or out of control. Eventually, she broke up with Jeff.

A few months later, she met David in school, she was nineteen. Kathy remembers her first impression was that he looked weird. He had a huge afro, which was his natural hair she later found out. However; this guy was always smiling and made her smile too. Their first date was bowling, it was fun. They dated for three months and David respected her and would only give her a kiss at the end of each date. Respect wasn't something she was used to; she'd never been treated with respect before.

Before long, Kathy met David's family and bonded with his youngest sister, Brenda. She was so easy to talk to and really listened to her. So did Dave, that was something Kathy wasn't used to either. It was nice to be heard. No one drank alcohol, got violent or abusive. They were a real family; another thing that was hard for Kathy to get used to.

Kathy had to adjust to these people; as everyone seemed to be so happy. Laughter was always present and Dave's family did things together. Weekends were planned for park outings, bingo, and games together, such as cards. Kathy married Dave upon high school graduation.

After living together for three years, Dave proposed. Life was good, until Kathy started to have "flashbacks", like PTSD, she began to remember sexual assaults, even as far back as age seven when a man had violated her, while her mother was passed out on the bed.

Dave was supportive, he knew her story, and he set out to find her the right help. Sex was always something Kathy dreaded; almost painful and not enjoyable. They both went to sex counselors and were given exercises to do to go slow, they worked together. After her son was born, a lot of the pain associated with sex was gone, but she never enjoyed it ever. Kathy began to "fake it" just to "get it over with." Dave was in the Army and never home; eight months out of the year he was gone.

Kathy loved her son, Ryan; he was her heart and soul; her only child. She grew used to doing everything while Dave was away and although she would show Ryan pictures of his father and he'd call him "da da", it would be difficult once Dave came home. Ryan would be scared of dad, he'd cry and be visibly upset, actually scared of him. It was hard on Dave, her, and Ryan.

They lasted seven years and then they began talking about divorce once he came home. The strain of time apart took its toll on their marriage; sex was hard to get into. It was as if they were in a brother and sister relationship. Although neither cheated, Kathy felt it would eventually lead to that, so they both decided divorce was the right thing to do.

Both went to the library and got children's books to educate Ryan on what was about to happen. Kathy and Dave met with their lawyers on base. Actually, they were both talking and laughing when both of their lawyers looked at each other and asked, "Are you sure you want to get divorced?" It was an amicable divorce.

To this day they are friends. Kathy will always have a ton of respect for him. Dave got her help right away in their relationship, he listened and believed her story; her life. He gave her a son and she thank God for that. Ryan is her reason she's here; her hope for the future; her bright star in the darkness. Kathy's words, "I love him so much and would die for him in a heartbeat. He's the only one who knows what my heart sounds like from the inside. He came from me, my son, my life."

Another ongoing quest for Kathy was to find out who her father was. Ever since we were little girls, she knew she looked different. She had long, straight, dark hair and almond eyes and medium stature; whereas I was blonde, blue eyed, and tall. It was our own grandfather who had yelled at the dinner table that "She was not a Hebb anyway." It was from that day on she tried desperately to find out who her father was.

After receiving a letter from Thelma Brown, who was from Tennessee and was our cousin from our mother's side, Robbie Lee Campbell, she claimed to have information on Kathy's father. That began the search and Kathy finally reached out to write to her mother in Florida. At the time, I was already living in Florida, after moving down after graduation.

In her twenty-one page letter, Kathy poured out everything. It was not easy to write, and she never knew she could hate someone as much as she did our mother. To Kathy's astonishment, Robbie wrote back and answered most of the questions to the best of her ability. Kathy found out that our mother started drinking at age fourteen and her own parents were alcoholics, so the cycle kept going.

Kathy decided to stop that cycle; she does drink but she has never been drunk in her life. It scares her; she continues to be a social drinker, maybe one or two drinks, then sticks to either water or soda.

So with a somewhat strange detached relationship with our mother, a woman Kathy has grown to despise, a woman who has given up her own children, Kathy made trips to Florida to visit me and see our mother. She was hoping to hear about her own biological father. However; our mother refused to talk about him; everything was hush hush. Even our father wouldn't say anything.

After her divorce, Kathy was working as a CNA when she and Ryan settled in a small apartment below the University of New Brunswick overlooking the water. One day her girlfriend Jackie called and they both met up so that their children could play and go swimming. It was there where she first met Rich. She was instantly attracted. However, Ryan didn't like him from the get-go. He was French and a smooth talker; she fell head over heels in love with him.

Later, she'd find out he was a player and had a narcissistic personality. He always knew the right things to say and do to make up and win her heart. So for a while it was an on again, off again relationship. He soon grew tired of her, and then went with other women, then back to her. Kathy became depressed and was taking pills to sleep. She soon turned into a detective, trying to find out where Rich was, who he was with, and why he was doing this. She was losing herself, and Ryan was losing her too.

At this point, Kathy felt like her life was falling apart and she wasn't adequately there for Ryan, so she spoke to Dave and he agreed to take him until she could get back on her feet. It was a hard decision to make, but she wanted him to be in a stable environment. She wrote Ryan back and forth and moved away from Rich.

Kathy eventually moved into an apartment and had two other girls as roommates. She was still working as a nurse's aide. Then months later, Rich called wanting to marry her and move to Montreal to meet his family. Kathy listened and her belly did another flip. Although her roommates said to hang up, she met him to just talk. He wined and dined her, brought her flowers, and said all the right things. They'd eventually marry and it lasted thirteen years. She'd hold onto this toxic relationship; anything so as not to be alone. She knew that her fear of abandonment was imminent.

Through it all, Ryan graduated high school with honors. Although moving to Montreal had isolated Kathy, mostly because of the language barrier, in the end it was good for Ryan. If she hadn't moved to Montreal, Ryan would never have pursued his passion of becoming a DJ, for which he is well-known in Montreal and makes a living doing so now.

Mistakes were made, but again her upbringing had made her susceptible to attracting or targeting a person with a narcissistic behavior. Kathy felt conflicted, confused, not ever experiencing the traditional harmonious family relationship, as normal families do. It is easy to fall prey to a smooth easy manipulative person with narcissistic traits like Rich.

All in all, Kathy had to step back and regroup and reflect on her own life choices. She also had to address "the issues" and begin to walk on a clearer path to find peace and resolution.

Kathy's wedding day:
Grandfather and Kathy (aged 23) Norma and myself (aged 20)

Reflection

One cannot change, One cannot grow...
Inside, without looking at the "ugly parts"...
I know ~ that weigh deep within my painful heart...
etched, engrained from an early start ~
that fester like a deep cut that doesn't heal...
I must face these emotions, I must conquer in order to heal ~
to learn is to grow, to break the cycle is harder to show ~
what I've learned and not repeat...
for life's lessons were bitter ~
but now are so sweet.

My thoughts: I must drop denial and accept accountability for my actions and my life. My parents, being alcoholics were not the best role models. How could they be? They were broken themselves. It's so important not to follow the earlier patterns of your life. It's even more important not to turn those patterns into habits, and have those habits become your character. I know it is not easy to break apart distant echoes—but it can be done. Only when you fall and lay still and listen, listen with all the truth that you have in you … will you find grace.

Chapter 16
Echoes

It is in this grace period that I now sit, listening to the echoes of my life, wondering which ones to listen to, which ones that are important enough to write down here.

Confused, I go to the dictionary and look up the word ECHO.

1. Repetition of a sound by reflection of sound waves from the surface
2. Any repetition or imitation of something, as of the opinions, actions, speech or dress of another.
3. The repetition of a musical note or certain sounds or syllables in poetry.

And suddenly I begin to understand from the definition of the word echo, from digging deeper into things, what those echoes have meant to me since childhood. They are repetitions of someone else's opinions, actions and speech. They are why I love the repetition of certain musical notes, certain sounds and syllables in my poetry, why I spend countless hours writing down the sound waves of my mind. Yes, for sure - echoes are the ghost in the machinery.

I was just thinking it's been six years since I've been divorced; when in fact, its actually only been three years. It's funny how time moves through our lives, slowing down and then other times speeding up, depending on past and future repetitions of actions, patterns and habits. Depending on those echoes.

It was in fact January 27th, 2016 when my divorce became final. I can still remember the mixture of feelings I had. In no way would I have imagined that our separation in 2011 would take five years before it was over and we were finally divorced. It was during those five years that my world came crashing down. Everything that I was accustomed to ended; I became a single mother; all of it was so overwhelming.

There were days that I was on autopilot and just managing to get by. My boys were eight and fifteen. As a mother, I overcompensated wanting to give them everything. In fact, looking back I realize how much I was drowning as I tried to be a life preserver for all of us. My oldest remembers more. He remembers the arguing, shouting and frustration that went on over the drinking.

Once I became pregnant at age 40, I remember thinking that drinking would break our marriage over time. It would be Zac's note on the fridge that read, "Dad, please stop drinking beer," that would silence the craziness for a while. Nathan would be born and be sheltered from the effects for 5 years as his father celebrated 5 years of sobriety. He would later relapse again telling Zac, 11 years at the time, "I'm going to start drinking again but don't tell your mom."

Addiction is the demon that steals the happiness from life and in turn one addiction can lead to another. It was just another disturbing fact and my boys would find our world turned upside down once my divorce was finalized. I'd need to find "Heather" again, and look through the narcissistic behavior that had been inflicted on my children.

As I tried to figure out a strategy to give my children consistency and restore normalcy to their lives, I fought hard. I had one attorney while he hired a total of three as the war raged on. I became the yard-keeper, house-keeper, handyman, a jack of all trades. I continued to juggle the many jobs, including being a mother and nurse. It was exhausting, but I kept going.

It was as if I was on a merry-go-round, a ride that never ended and I couldn't get off. At the time, I was working as a RN at an urgent care. With the 12-hour shifts and the stress of a divorce that dragged on, I finally broke and gave them my two week notice. I was having problems sleeping, and in an effort to deal with the ongoing stress I joined a gym. Over the next few years, I'd go from weighing 170 pounds to weighing 130 pounds. "The divorce diet," I'd call it.

It was quite a shock to remember me before my divorce. Only after my children were sleeping, would I retire in my chair to eat and watch Nancy Grace. I never realized how depressed I was back then. Now I never watch TV. I don't wear big baggy clothes, and I don't watch the Nancy Grace show. At the time, the Casey Anthony story was airing and dragging on for months on end.

With my divorce finalized on January 27th, 2016; it was time to move forward with my life. Today, my boys and I remain in the marital lake house; a place we have called home for twenty-nine years. I started a new job as a rehab nurse at work, it is easier to forget my hectic schedule and focus just on my patients.

Being a nurse is a humbling job, as I'm able to see patients progress over weeks of intense rehab reach goals so they can return home or be transferred to another skilled facility. It takes an empathetic heart seeing, listening, and feeling their frustration as they relearn to feed, dress, and bathe themselves and learn to walk again.

I've been an RN for twenty-eight years with thirteen years working at the hospital on a busy med-surg oncology floor. Over time, I've had my share of patients who have died. It's never easy to lose a patient. I remember each one of them, their medical issues, their families and their circumstances.

For those on hospice, it's an end of life decision and it's about comfort, care, and keeping the patient comfortable until the end of life. As I administer pain medication to them, I know I'm doing the right thing to ease their pain, and to reduce their anxiety. Eventually, I know the morphine I'm administering will slowly depress the CNS and effect the area of the brain that tells them to breathe and inevitably they will not take that last breath and they will die. It's not easy to see a family grieving as I assure them their loved one was in no pain; showing them compassion, consoling them, hugging them, and just being there crying with them.

I will never forget when my grandmother, also known as "mom," died. My son Zac was 5 years old and it was hard for me to leave him for the first time. I flew to Canada, hoping to make it before she passed. I did not, but my sister Kathy was there with my Aunt Helen. It was hard to see her that way, we cried and consoled one another. When her nurse came in later, I spoke with her and she assured me she was not in any pain when she passed. When someone dies it's important to treat the body with dignity, respect, and compassion. I informed her nurse that I also was an RN and I would remove her lines to prepare her to go to the morgue. I removed her IV line, all dressings, and her Foley catheter. I washed her body, so she was clean and graced her presence in a dignified manner. I made sure her eyes were closed and folded her hands on her chest, so she appeared to be sleeping. Afterwards, I also tucked a small rolled towel under her chin to keep her mouth closed as rigor mortis would be setting in soon.

Kathy and I said our goodbyes to Aunt Helen and stayed a while just sitting with "mom." We spoke of her hard life, the abuse and pain she endured over the years. Now Norma Kathleen Hebb was finally at rest. She had enjoyed 17 peaceful years after our grandfather died.

Now as I work in a facility that has a geriatric long-term care on one side and a skilled rehab on the other, many of my long-term patients are fond of me and ask, "Are you going to be my nurse today?" I treat them just like family and I give them the respect they deserve. Nursing is a selflessness profession for I am there to serve those in need. Although it is hectic and crazy at times as a floor nurse, just hearing that one say "Thank you, I'm glad I have you as my nurse today" is what keeps me going now.

Reflection

To love yourself is to find yourself...

For 27 years I lived my life for others, caught up in the rat race of living, being a wife, mother and nurse, I filled many roles. Perhaps, I spent many years putting everyone's needs first and in doing so I lost "me". A separation and final divorce gave me another chance to look at my life ... a shift from the ordinary brought me to a life of extraordinary ... a difficult journey with many twists and turns, but I realized I needed to take a good look at myself ... Fears, tears, sleepless nights brought me closer to finding the real me, no longer lost I found the young girl who could smile, laugh, and see how wonderful life could be ... dancing, music, interacting with friends, keeping fit ... I nurtured myself to love myself AS IS, to value me and realize I'm worthy of love, not merely existing anymore but truly LIVING ... I know something will grow from all you have been through ... It will be YOU ...

Reflection

Why do memories bleed?
It's as if the planted seed has erupted to bloom,
but yet... it seems too soon
the tears that flow, I do not know...
why it can't be
but really if I stop to see,
I've changed so much from who I use to be...
I can't say I knew the way
but like a tree that remains still,
grounded deep,
it won't bend until...
.the harsh winds and rain do fall,
the limbs will bend,
the tree could fall
but I chose to withstand the storm...
to navigate my way,
to be reborn...
I'm not any different from you,
but in my heart I decided to...
find my way out to make it somehow...
the best I could
I'm standing now.

Reflection

A nurse's promise

I walk with them all, no judgement on class, race or religion ... they just want to be heard, to be validated, to be understood. Who am I to question their beliefs? I have so much to learn from them ... they are vulnerable, they are weak, relying on me for the answers, my response might not be what they want to hear, it's hard to listen to the spoken word, the spoken truth. That's what I do, and in doing so, it allows me to accept ... everything ... in context, for we are human and not everything is in our control ... we must be open to listening and accepting. Live life each day with a grateful heart. Have no regrets and be kind to one another. We are not invisible, but share so much in common really, we must find peace and love with one another unified.

As a nurse, it is humbling to serve others, to see them at their weakest to become stronger, heal and move further on their own to regain their independence, to persevere. But, in some cases, there is that moment when there is nothing more that can be done, and then it's about being there for the patient and the family as they move through the grieving process to accept the end of life as it comes ... to just to be there for them.

Chapter 17
The Divorce

I can recall a moment when I was going through family photos of how peaceful the house was. The serenity was beautiful as the sun was streaming through the front window. The chaos, the anger, and tension was finally gone. It was then that I felt totally alone, totally empty. It was an eerie feeling and I began to think how much my boys depended on me.

For a moment I felt like the traumatized child awaiting for someone to save me, but in fact it would be myself who would need to do that. That's when I felt the heaviness, uneasiness as I faced my own fears. The tears rolled down my face; it was all up to me; the financial bills, all the chores, house repairs, everything. But deep down inside I knew I could do it; it was just a matter of learning, prioritizing, and moving forward. Time would tell, I just had to take it one day at a time.

The most difficult part of divorce for me was the shared custody of the boys. Primarily, much harder for Nathan, being younger it was difficult on him. He also had to get used to a blended family once his father announced his engagement a few weeks after our divorce was finalized. Zac was older and he eventually moved in with me once he was driving.

I sought professional counseling for all of us, after Nathan began acting out. There'd be phone calls from the teachers at school and experimentation with drugs and self-harm. Although I knew the reason why; my words and knowledge could not penetrate; he had to hear it from another professional not his mother. It was family therapy, my boys and I went for several sessions. It helped us on our road to healing and recovery.

As a mother, my boys are my everything. They came first and I vowed there'd be no one else replacing their dad. Once I started dating and going out, I was careful and selective with whom they would meet. I have to say I enjoyed my new found freedom. I became a gym enthusiast and weighing 130 pounds it made me feel confident and sure of myself. It felt good to be attractive to men again. However, dating and being single at age fifty was definitely difficult.

For me, it was liberating to be in control of my life; my decisions, my plans, I was free. Over the years, my boys adjusted too. Zachary at age twenty entered the Navy Boot Camp, he worked hard but was sent home after eight weeks of training. He was hospitalized for Norwalk Virus, which set him back and his discharge listed Separation Anxiety. Zac age twenty-one has since returned to college full time to obtain his Associate of Arts degree. He has a part-time job and works weekends.

Nathan, age fifteen is in grade 10; he's in Honors English and is thinking of becoming a nurse someday. They are both my backbone and help me out with chores around the house. As I speak now, Nathan is typing my words and has done so since the beginning of chapter one. I am so thankful for that.

We are open and honest and talk about everything,.my boys know there's nothing we cannot discuss. Every opportunity I get, I remind them of peer pressure and not to be persuaded to get into drinking, drugging, and other addictions. They know how much it has cost me and our entire family and how they are genetically predisposed.

Zachary remembers how his "gaming addiction" cost him a lot and he has had to face the failures that came with it. Many missed opportunities in personal growth and maturity along with lack of social inadequacy has delayed him. His awareness now keeps him from losing himself in the "game world" again. He is now a valid contributor to the new Tampa Bay Vipers XFL fan advisory network. He enjoys writing his blog there. I am very proud of him.

Even my boys noticed how I've changed. I have begun to live life again, not merely existing; no longer the enabler, I'm happy again. They mentioned that I was in my "Midlife crisis" as I began to go out dancing and socializing more. I would meet many men; the young ones were all about the fun, love and leave em', the older men were "wanting to take care of me." It was challenging to find the right companionship.

Then one weekend, a mutual friend of ours, Rob introduced me to Phil. He was different from anyone I knew; interesting and someone I wanted to know more about. He hardly drank, and never touched a cigarette in his life. He was attentive, always there for me; I felt safe and he accepted me as is. He listened to my story; he knew my life and never judged. He opened my heart again with the love of music.

I had to let go of that desperate need to rescue someone, for ultimately that was no longer my purpose. This was a need that resulted from dysfunctional relationships only, and had caused me to neglect myself. Now it was about taking care of me and loving me fiercely, for that would in fact attract someone who appreciated my worth and someone who wouldn't take advantage of my kindness.

Again, the word "relationship" would be a focus for me. I came to realize that I must truly love myself before I let someone else alter that. It was in the absence of myself, that left a hole in my soul; how could I love another if I felt this emptiness inside? Only after peeling back the painful layers could I begin to heal. That took honest effort and commitment; not easy to do but so grateful I did. I realized nothing outside of myself would bring me that fulfilling feeling, so I knew it was time to let him into my heart.

Phil (my partner of 5 years) compliments me; he doesn't need to complete me entirely. We both bring our pasts into our own relationship, but that too balances us. I have learned to be responsible just for me and not for other people's problems that I did not cause. His patience and love has helped me immensely and the music he has brought into my life illuminates it. I will never forget when Phil took me to see Rush on their R-40 Tour at the Amalie Arena. I had been a fan my entire life and as a teenager dreamed of seeing this Canadian band. Unknown to anyone, this tour in 2015 would be their last. We both hold onto that memory, it was astounding, and I will forever be grateful to Phil who made it happen.

I still experience times when I feel anxious, but I'm sure childhood echoes of fear and trauma facilitated that. My issues with trust can create problems that aren't really there. Again, I'm aware of the "whys" I feel this way; the need to close off my heart and thus to protect myself. Phil shows me complete trust and allows me to talk about it, which is therapeutic for both of us. Sometimes I think he fills in the pieces that I lost when I was child. I believe we all have insecurities at times that we can bring in from time to time. Healing is lifelong.

Phil enabled me to find myself; the girl who loved living, dancing, and had a spark for life restored by music again. We have experienced many special moments, concerts, places, and travel. I am thankful for that. I just needed his kindness and effort to make me shine again.

November is now upon us and the weather is much cooler with thanksgiving only days away. Being a nurse, I had to choose a winter holiday to work and this year with our custody arrangement my boys will be with their father and in-laws on thanksgiving. Since Phil will be away on a scheduled trip, I will be working this thanksgiving, but I'm so thankful for Christmas as we will all be together then. Holidays are a time to be with those you love, to make memories and live every moment as life is short and unpredictable. I'm forever thankful for my boys, my sister, my friends, and Phil each and every day for life is a blessing.

Myself, my two boys, and Phil

Reflection

I gave you my heart,
I gave it to you...
to protect and hold,
we were devoted to...
that first kiss,
my hand in yours,
I whispered to you,
"my love is so true"
Forgive me for doubting you
I was broken inside,
I questioned our love and just wanted to hide...
you allowed me to go,
but inside you did know...
I would find nothing
"that would last"
and tearfully I knew,
I could always rely onto...
your lasting touch,
your words were for me
"I'll let you run in order to see"
the strength that took from you,
I know...
showed perpetual trust in order to let go...
and now I see all you are to me
was there beautifully all along
holding you,
I look in your eyes to see
that keeps me devoted to "us"
for it all began with love and trust.

Reflection

Pouring in poison can taint a sweet heart
sprinkling and spilling seeds of insecurity and doubt
festering to grow and to ultimately destroy,
what you both have too
standing as a wall of anger,
it can distance you.
false accusations
jealousy can hurt like hell,
for once spoken from your mouth,
it can sting as well
penetrating deep like a thorn in the skin,
rupturing and bleeding
it sabotages everything within
ghosts from the past,
insecurities too
revelations from the heart
try to swallow you
digging deep inside you,
you must look to see
working through undeserving,
shameful parts of you
you deserve love
nurturing and hearing the words
"I love you"

Reflection

My Thanksgiving Wish

Thankfulness comes from deep within,
for this moment will never be again
it's not what you "get"
but what you "give"
and much like the grateful life you live
from day to day,
hold onto that gratitude,
it will only grow more inside of you
spreading warmth to smiles on faces
perhaps it's as if to say,
there's no price to give of you,
in everything you say and do
a person of their worth, hold onto
their love is true.
So today,
with pumpkin smells in the air,
tasty treats and food to share
remember those who have passed
and are up above,
it's a time to be with those you love
and embrace today,
for love is a wide open heart,
that has no restraints to hold onto
the more you "give",
the more "love" will be showered on you.

Chapter 18
The Revelation

It's December and the holiday season will soon be upon us. As I sit here now going through pictures, my mind goes back to my father who died.

I think about how things might have been if only alcoholism hadn't affected my father's life and his father before him. Would we have all been happy or like a "normal" family? Now, as I'm older I know in my heart that it was the alcohol that destroyed us. The dictionary defines alcohol as being a colorless, volatile, flammable, liquid produced by the natural fermentation of sugars.

The word "volatile" as it applies to drinking accurately defines how alcohol can cause a sudden radical change, an explosive temper, or behavior that gets out of control. I can still hear the yelling, screaming, and see the anger on my parents faces when they fought in front of us. These words alcohol, volatile, radical changes all describe the vivid memory I have of my father and grandfather when they were drunk.

Their behavior made me fearful, unsure, and anxious. Only now, as I look back on my own life and my children's upbringing, can I appreciate how difficult parenting can be. I can say it's important to balance your life in order to deal with those stressful times with child rearing. It's not a bad thing to have a drink or two, but it's important to accept the responsibility for drinking. If impaired, refrain from driving and putting anyone else at risk from your own wrong doings. It's important to keep in place effective stress relievers that don't revolve around alcohol. Mine now includes gardening, music, and most importantly writing.

Now at fifty-six, I can make more sense of my earlier years. My parents ineffective coping mechanisms of alcohol abuse had only managed to cripple us, stealing memorable family functions and denying us a childhood. After my own divorce, I could see that alcoholism had destroyed my marriage.

It would take me years to finally forgive my father, grandfather, and my ex-husband. It was necessary to forgive in order to release myself from the pain. It didn't mean that everything that was done by that person was okay, it just meant I came to find peace by letting it go. By forgiving them, it didn't mean I needed to reconnect with them or have them in my life anymore. I needed to move forward with my own life.

Being estranged from my father for fifteen years only added to the inability to bond, and in my younger years it was easier to think of him as dead. Since Kathy and I never heard from him, no Christmas presents in the mail, no birthday cards, no phone calls, no letters. Then, upon meeting him and being sexually assaulted by him in my twenties, I knew I would not wish to see or hear from him again. Because of this I did not want him in my children's life, and I did everything in my power to protect them. I wouldn't jeopardize their well-being by allowing him into my children's lives.

In order to finally find forgiveness, I had to come to terms with my anger and resentment. As a child I always felt it was my fault, something I did or caused. Eventually, my maturity enabled me to see it had nothing to do with me or my sister. An addictive personality was feeding their own needs; that by delivering alcohol to their body as a means of existing and rendering them helpless to be able to effectively parent children.

When my grandfather died, I did not go to the funeral. I could only feel relieved that my grandmother would finally be freed from his ongoing abuse. She'd finally find peace and serenity for seventeen years before her own death transpired. Only after my grandfather's death did Kathy came forth and tell our grandmother that we too had suffered sexual abuse at the hands of our grandfather, that was the reason I didn't attend the funeral. As I sit here now Christmas is just a few days away and I remember family, my memory always goes back to family. I can still recall when I heard that my father had died.

It was my step-mother, Pam who called to say he was sick in the hospital. Soon after my dad returned home, he died shortly after from complications related to pneumonia. I can remember thinking "I should feel bad he has passed," but instead, I felt numb and indifferent. My emotions were mixed in with guilt for not feeling sad and angry that he was such a bad person. I did not attend his funeral either.

Once I reconnected with my half-brother, Christopher, I'd find out that my Aunt Meleta was the reason he had moved to Florida and she died on the very same day my father did. As I pick up this photo and look, I see my father embracing Aunt Meleta in the hospital after suffering a stroke. Ironically, she'd return home and a week later die from a massive heart attack. Christopher reached out to me on Facebook when I was in the midst of my divorce. He familiarized his life with mine as he was also separated and divorcing. He wanted to get full custody of his 2 boys since his wife was an alcoholic and drug addict. Again, I'd hear about the familiar affects that addiction had cost him too. Christopher, I would find out became a father at age 16; dropping out of school to work and take care of his financial burdens. He was devastated from the loss of his father and aunt.

Christopher would eventually get his GED and marry having two more boys to raise. I'd get the news again from Facebook that my half-brother Christopher passed away in his sleep. He had a heart attack and was just 49.

Before he died, we had last spoke on the phone just before Easter. I regret not meeting up with him and his boys. But the family dysfunction was the reason I didn't want to keep in touch over the years. I wasn't comfortable bringing extended family members into my children's lives after mine had been so traumatic. Breaking the cycle of alcoholism has cost me valuable time, heartache and moments I can't get back.

I have finally forgiven myself and my family including my ex-husband. It hasn't been easy but it was necessary for me. If I had continued to hold onto the bitterness it would have eaten me alive from the inside out like a cancer. By letting go of the anger, I could release that hold on me and eliminate myself from being a victim and restore peace in my life. However painful it was to go back, to remember, to feel, to write this book, it was actually my healing grace. I could finally accept that other people's behavior had more to do with their own internal struggles and really had nothing to do with me and my sister. That in itself is healing.

Now, as we gather around the Christmas tree, I'm humbled, blessed, and so grateful to have both of my sons, Phil, his mother Melissa, Third Wheel, a blind cat, and Sophie a 12-year-old German Shepard here with me. Christmas will never be about the gifts; it is so much more than that. I am the richest person ever to be in the company of those I love. It is the peaceful blessings of Christmas that enriches my heart for better things than the things I've left behind me.

It seems that this Christmas has brought me closer to God, to peace. I pray that the days to come will bring me and my family joy, trust, and gratitude, and that sorrow, anxiety, and complaining are a thing of the past. Merry Christmas, everyone!

Phil's dog "Sophie"
posed in front of the Christmas tree

Reflection

I love the rain...
I love the storms...
I love the darkness
from which I was born.
The monstrous strength from lightning I hear...
as thunderstorms erupt
I do not fear...
the winds strong as they can be...
whipping limbs and breaking them from the tree...
the calmness of the storm will come
and then the light will beam to guide me there...
I've chosen life,
no defeat here
for perseverance I've grown from
and my energy grows with the beaming sun...
for light will always help you find...
truth and love in due time
hang onto hope and feed it everyday
and just believe in life,
it's the only way
it's the circle of life,
it will go on and on...
hang onto it,
watch it build you up and make you strong
for in its grip it holds you there...
to live and breathe...
for this I pray
you see your worth,
your value,
your truth today...

Reflection

What are you hiding?
Is it working for you?
Is it holding you back?
What are you holding onto?
You can be so much more,
your confidence can grow
if only you can see it...
and let the rest go
Are you truly happy?
Have you pushed yourself to...
stand on the edge
and reach onto...
any goal is possible,
but you must convince your mind so...
the world is ready and waiting for you
now just let go.

Reflection

Let the thoughts come,
let the words flow
covering the white paper, in dark ink...
let go ~ releasing those feelings,
causing them to rip and scrape your heart...
tearing away pieces,
gradually bleeding...
they break apart ~ revealing a truth,
a known scripture from within...
a cleansing,
a beginning,
a middle
and an end
regurgitating,
remembering...
gradually erupting from inside
let the truth release you from all those demons you hide...

Reflection

It will never be about the number of gifts under the tree...
take the time to look deep,
into that person to see...
their loves,
their thrills,
the things that make them feel...
Alive inside...
for that will be the GIFT,
the joy,
the specialness that's derived from...
never the cost,
but your vested time...
you spent to... GIVE them the GIFT...
from your heart...
from you.

As we frantically shop for that perfect "Christmas gift", we should all remember gifts are not what makes Christmas. The most meaningful, memorable gift will be the one that brings a smile to someone's face, and a cherished moment or memory to their HEART. Something that costs very little, but only takes love, time, and presence.

Chapter 19

The Discovery

New Year's Eve and I watch time drifting toward the year 2020. Now time is something I'm aware of. Throughout all of man's experience, through every aspect of the world and universe he or she inhabits, runs the elusive entity called time.

Time governs not merely our activities, but our very being. Of all the great abstractions of science, it is omnipresent time – space or force or matter – that comes most often to our lips. Time is a great teacher, a great healer; it stands still, slips away from us or flies past us. We can save time or lose it, spend time or waste it, even beat it or kill it.

What we cannot do, oddly enough, is define it. As the New Year approaches, I'm so excited as I count down the days. I'm happy and grateful for I'm finally nearing completion of my book. My heart feels full; it's taken me two years to put into words my sister's life and mine, and to find order, meaning, and resolution from our chaotic, crazy upbringing with our alcoholic parents. I feel a sense of fulfilment and finality, for I've written from my heart pouring out well-kept family secrets in order to find meaning and close that door and finally move on. In my efforts, I hope that others who can relate can also rise above any loss that alcohol has caused them. Most importantly, in doing so, to remember that you are your own person, not defined by your past, but purely your own self. Regardless of what music life plays for you, we must all choose how to dance to it.

It's just a few days away, 2020 is almost here and my thoughts are diverted to my sister. Only a few weeks short of her birthday, she received the most incredible news. I remember the day she called me to say she had finally discovered who her real father was. She had been looking for her father her entire life and now time had given her this opportunity to know. She'd finally get the answers after a good friend Murray McDonnell brought back her DNA kit results. It was a long time coming, Kathy would finally be able to piece her life together and begin the process of locating lost relatives, find answers she had always dreamed of knowing. What a beautiful gift she had received, and with the new year, new changes and new beginnings had come to bless her.

As she spoke to me on the phone, she'd tell me that she had found out that her father's name was Donald O. Lininger and he was born on May 10th, 1931 in Iowa, USA and died on June 10th, 1976. She learned that he had hired our mother, Robbie Lee Campbell to be his caregiver when his health had declined. Unknown to the Lininger family, and to Donald himself, she'd become pregnant with his child.

Kathy had found out by emailing her first cousin, Wayne Tietz, who her own father still had a living sister in Largo, FL who just turned 90 going by the name "Gertrude." She also found out that her father and our mother lived in a house twenty minutes from my current house in the Land O' Lakes area for about a year, until Robbie Lee left Donald taking his last $3,500 before Donald moved back to Iowa. Hearing of this fact, some Lininger family members don't think nicely of Robbie and her greed and has left a bad taste in their mouths.

It's strange that Kathy and I both had different fathers, yet we were both profoundly affected by alcoholism. Robbie Lee would eventually meet my father, Richard Hebb, they'd be married, and Kathy's biological father would be kept a secret for all those years. Alcohol would blur the truth from ever being told until finally at age 58, Kathy would learn the secret. She'd eventually see a photo of Donald and a mirror image that resembled her, especially the eyes would seal her discovery of who her real father was.

Although our mother Robbie Lee had given Kathy life, she had never given her the answers she knew, that Kathy truly wanted. However; neither did Richard, they had kept those secrets and took them to their graves. Now time alone allowed the story to be known. I'm so grateful that I can be writing this in my book. What a wonderful Christmas present to her and an astounding new year awaits her as she traces her family background and becomes acquainted to relatives she has never known.

In a sense, she is saddened that her father Donald never knew she existed and that he died at such a young age. Kathy mourns the father she never knew. She'd learn that Donald suffered greatly throughout his short life. He had contracted a severe infection that spread throughout his body. He had arthritis as a young man, which had gotten worse with age. His joints would literally cease up and he had a shuffling gate. In his late 30's he contracted tuberculosis and eventually died at the age of 45.

Upon finding her first cousins named Wayne and Don Tietz, she found out that a book had been written about Don Tietz called "One American Dreamer" by Alice C. Bateman. It is during this period that her father and Robbie Lee were together, and Don Tietz was a police officer in Tampa. She is presently reading the novel, a wonderful time for her, looking back and becoming acquainted with a family she never knew.

I'm overjoyed for Kathy; she went from a small family to learning she has over four hundred relatives. 2020 will be her year to make peace with her past and to discover new things waiting for her. It's been overwhelming news; the void she had always felt is no longer there. She will no doubt be paying a visit to Algona, Iowa where many of her extended family resides now and are waiting to meet her.

As I talk to her on the phone, I asked her about her new year resolution. She speaks of finding peace and hope and to replace doubt with love. Kathy hopes to discover renewed strength, to overcome the fear from her past and to move into the new year with good health and happiness. On December 25th, her one and only son Ryan announced his engagement to be married and that also brought her an immense amount of joy, as she overcomes the fear from her past and moves into the new year.

For me, this year has been a busy and productive one. I've worked hard to complete what I set out to do and I'm looking forward to finishing my book. It has come full circle, remembering my childhood, to think back, and reliving those feelings and that turbulence, and jotting it down on paper and releasing it. It has been self-cleansing. I've also been blessed to have two wonderful boys, a boyfriend, family and friends to support me with my endeavors.

Even at work as a nurse, I'm humbled to be able to give my patients the best of care. As New Year's Eve grows closer, I remember my patient, Miriam. She has been a dialysis patient for ten years, so she is well versed on her medical care. Although her dialysis is imperative to remaining alive, she strives to take control of her life and in doing so, she rebels at times, being non-compliant. I listen to her explaining that she has a 3-4-hour chair time for her dialysis to be finished and is upset that with the Christmas and holiday hours, her scheduled appointment has been changed. I reach out to her with selflessness to listen and comfort her as she must go on New Year's Eve, as the dialysis center will be closed on New Year's Day. I can empathize with her as she is not planning to undergo dialysis at this time as she hopes to be spending time with visitors at her bedside.

I reason with her and she finally agrees to go to the outpatient center to return afterwards, and I explained that she could have New Year's Day with her family. She agrees. That made me happy to act as her patient advocate and to see that she understood it's imperative to go.

It is here and on New Year's Day that my resolutions are simple. Life changes. We all suffer loss, but we learn to love stronger. 2020 is here and I pray only for good health, for a life that is rich in laughter, knowledge, family, friends and love. I vow to work harder to be a better person, to give back to others, and to always be grateful. With hope and a positive mindset, any and all achievements are possible. Just remember we are all worthy, perfect just the way we are.

Happy New Year, Cheers and Blessings to you all.

Reflection

It's incredible how time is ... as much as you grow you will never know ... everything ... that's how it goes, for it is to be that way; in order that you can process and see those things that matter can only be ... loved and missed ... find time to look deeper inside you, let go of those things that don't count ... reconnect, give value to those who know you best and have always rose ... to the occasion to be at your side, although far away, really not so, for they will always be with you, will never let go ... they live in your heart, forever so ...

Reflection

Give back, you will always be ahead...
ONE small gesture can be the world to someone else.
ONE kind word can break the silence that holds them back.
ONE open mind can build the trust to move forward again.
ONE listening ear can be the new beginning to restore hope.
ONE feeling touch can inspire faith to push on...
ONE person,
ONE hand,
ONE moment can make the difference,
hold judgement for others and see with your heart,
we are not so different;
unite and be there...
for one another.

Reflection

Flying and floating and hovering to dance...
never insignificant,
but purely by chance
I gaze upon the colors ... so vibrant and clear...
orange, brown and checkered, with a wingspan, so near
I'm amazed with its presence ... landing alone,
secure with its beauty, it stands solely alone
a lifespan so short and merely just days...
but owning that moment ~ I'm filled with such praise...
You own your own presence...
I feel it, I know...
your black n' white pattern and sunset glow
your time is short, so beautifully defined...
not one to be forgotten,
but to resonate in my mind.

You are one of a kind ~ your own special you ... Be comfortable with who you are, your journey and where you are going ... time is fleeting, live everyday fully ... own your presence, you make an impression on those you meet everyday ... it shows beautifully ...

Reflection

To GIVE means more than to receive. GIVE your time, your attention, yourself ... to those who are needing, hurting or alone ... just listen with clarity, it costs nothing to be there ... but means so much to another.

Chapter 20
Peace Again

As the new year begins, I'm finally taking a deep breath; it's comforting to enjoy the solace after the holiday; to just look back on the year that has passed, to stop and reevaluate my goals and aspirations. My boys are home, out of school for winter holidays, so it's nice to catch up with them, relaxing with no fixed schedule or alarm clock ringing for a while. We can make plans for the movies, attend events, and just enjoy the extra sleeping in. I'm so blessed to be able to work PRN (as needed) as an RN, that enables me to make my own schedule, giving me available time for my boys to schedule appointments, take vacations, and attend events of our choosing.

I think back and I'm proud of what we have achieved; many changes over the four years since my divorce. But, the main and most prominent change is the peacefulness that has been restored in our house. It's crippling how much alcoholism can keep the selfish alcoholic from even noticing all the havoc their behavior costs every member of the family; and how hard it can be to put shattered lives back together again. However; we persevered to restore harmony to our lives and for me "peace" is sacred, and healing ongoing.

For that reason, it took me a long time to introduce Phil to my boys. It was important to me not to bring a man into my life that wouldn't be there for the duration. Phil is a man who held me up for the four years as my divorce drug on. He was there anytime of the day or night, just a phone call away. He's the one who brought music back into my life, lifting my spirit and showing me that I could smile and laugh again. He has introduced music to my boys giving them guitars for Christmas and showing them how to tune them. He set up a drum set in our front room so Nathan can practice.

As my birthday arrives, Phil surprised me by making the two-hour drive to be with me. Distance hasn't made it easy for us for the four years we've been together, but we've done it. Each compromising for the other, for that's what love is all about. Compromising, respect and trust, without one the other could not hold it all together. We have all enjoyed the walks with Sophie, his 12-year-old German Shepherd; his and our adored baby. We've all grown in those four years and I'm grateful for every moment we've been together.

For my January 7th birthday, we went out to dinner and shared a celebratory glass of red sangria, our evening was perfect, and I couldn't have asked for more; spending quality time alone was nice too, as my boys were out. The next day work schedules and commitments would send Phil home on his two-hour commute back to Orlando.

I'd find out later that Neil Peart died on my birthday, he was an incredible musician, a drummer for the legendary band Rush, a best-selling author, and a lyricist. It was his words in the song Limelight 1980 being "cast in this unlikely role, ill-equipped to act … One must put up barriers … To keep oneself intact," that resonated in my soul, as my sister and I have hidden behind secrets as a form of survival, but now no more. Again, it struck me hard to hear of Neil Peart's untimely death, Rush, a Canadian band that was there when I was just a teenager, listening, grasping on every word they sang. Those words brought me comfort during my life with an alcoholic grandfather.

I can only be thankful for being at their R40 show, later to find out this would be their very last tour in 2015. I will always be most grateful to Phil for taking me to see Rush for the first time, it brought me so much joy. If not for the music, I don't believe I'd be here. Once married, music became non-existent as I threw myself into being a wife, mother, a nurse always forgetting about me. Everything for everyone but losing myself in the mix. Only after I met Phil, did music reemerge and in fact was instrumental to my healing. Music, then and music now has always been medicine for my soul, music having the power to perinate and absorb into the very areas of pain my heart had endured. Music saved my life; music is life sustaining.

In order to break the cycle of three generations of alcoholism it was important for me to look deeply at myself, and deal with all the repressed feelings I felt, vowing to be better than what broke me inside. Instead of displacing my anger, or resentment, I now act from my heart, not from my pain. That's not always easy and sometimes I will catch myself, but again we are far from perfect and that's what makes us human.

Silence and secrets only protect the abuser ... But who is there to protect us? Repressed memories just cause guilt and shame to fester. Only when I could breathe life into my story could I put peace to my past by breaking the cycle; Kathy and I have become pillars of strength and worth. Life is never about existing, but all about living a life with purpose.

Breaking the cycle; work that goes on for a lifetime, knowledge and accountability to better oneself every day. I choose to be happy, to make good choices with an open and positive mindset, life will always give us surprises, but that's called living. I don't accept defeat, always finding strength to stand up again and again if needed. We should never underestimate our worth, our desire to learn goes on forever and in the end, there will emerge a better person. I am laying my pencil down now and the tears that roll down my face are those of happiness, for I have achieved my goal in finishing the book.

Reflection

Look upon a rose,
the stem is the anchor from where the bud grows...
the thorns sharp, and resilient protect the flower for show...
intricately made in beautiful colors of every shade...
pink, floral and fragrant, symbolic of you,
from where you have been and from where you grew...
no one can say you won't be remembered my dear,
for you are the flower that brought smiles to others, tears and
remembrance...
and with these words I say,
You are the rose that blooms today.

Never forget the humble beginnings and appreciate life's lessons that make you who you are today. A Rose is everlasting and memorable, each different, unique and beautiful. The stem being the foundation grounds you, the petals soft and delicate hold you, and the thorns sharp and resilient protect you.

All of us have journeys, but our past does not define us. Although abandoned as a child, I have always been a devoted mother, giving my boys everything, that I was capable of giving. But most importantly, I gave them love. I never grew up with caring parents, their addiction came first ... and the bottle clouded their judgement and ability to be good parents, I've survived neglect and abuse from parents, my grandfather and others, but regardless I have never let it hinder my growth. I studied hard to become an RN, mother of two, photographer and writer. My words are written to inspire others to push forward with their lives to, learn and let go of the past. And to LIVE LIFE to its fullest each and every day.

Reflection

Looking at the road ahead...
I gaze, I smile and nod my head.
I can't say it was so easy to do...
to walk along, I stumbled, but I grew
A smoother path up ahead I can see.
With the warm sun shining directly on me...
producing light that beams and glows,
illuminating the ways I chose to go...
humbled with grace, I'm grateful I've gone...
down this road that seemed to take so long
change was never easy to learn or do.
I had to look within myself, deep inside to
unlearn the things I learned from those I knew...
for they were family and wounded people too...

Survivors we are, children of alcoholics; but we have made tremendous strides in healing from all of the abuse and neglect. Until I went back, I couldn't make sense of it all, and now I'm able to put them to rest for once I healed myself, I can heal others. The hardest part is moving past the denial and deceit, and by accepting the truth, by dropping the shame and blame and seeing myself as the beautiful person, not the image that was engrained in me as a child. This is not the end of my story, but merely the beginning of a story yet to be told.

Acknowledgements

It was not an easy journey to take, to write my story, but it was necessary to do this "alone." Time has a way of reminding us that our own personal struggles are only a testimonial to our very being. In no way did my past "steal," my present. It has only made me more grateful for everything and everyone who has been there for me along the way.

My greatest supporter, my protector and shield; my sister Kathy Hebb made this book possible, thank you for your insight and urging me to go forward and write "our story." Also, I wish to thank Phil, my partner who said to me, "please write, tell your story, it needs to be told; it could benefit others."

I thank my sons Zachary and Nathan who supported my efforts to put my words on paper and format them for this book. It was their time and effort to help me type this for my editor; since I'm slow at typing compared to them.

Lastly, I'm forever grateful to Ken Eulo a bestselling author, the editor of my book who said to me, "I don't need to tell you how to write; just don't go back and change your words, keep going forward as you have your entire life." Your belief in me was the fuel behind the fire and I'll always be thankful to him for seeing my potential even when I had doubts. Much thanks to my family and friends in Canada and friends here in the States, who were behind me for the two long years it took to write this book. Thanks guys, and much love to all.

About the Author

Heather Stoker was born in Tampa, Fl and lived most of her childhood in Liverpool, N.S, Canada. She began writing as a troubled teen having a poem featured in "Pandora's Box in Nova Scotia" at the age of 17. She graduated a year later from Liverpool Regional High School in 1981. Upon graduation she moved back to Florida at age 18 to pursue a career in the medical field. In 1983 she became a certified dental assistant before branching off into nursing becoming a Licensed Practical Nurse in 1993. She was a member of  National Vocational Technical Honor Society with perfect attendance. She furthered her education in 1996 achieving an Associates in Science Degree for Nursing R.N./HONORS. In her experience as an R.N. she worked on the med surg/oncology at Florida Hospital. Eventually she shifted her career path into Urgent Care Facilities, Vaccine Clinics, and is now currently working at a Skilled Rehab/Long-Term Care Facility specializing in Gerontology.

Her Hobbies include gardening, photography, and nurturing animals. She is a mother of two and lives in a spacious lake-front home that gives her the inspiration for her writing. Her mission is to continue writing for those who cannot step forward and speak for themselves on topics relating to abandonment, loss, heartbreak, neglect, and abuse. She inspires to be the voice of the voiceless and carry her message to everyone who needs to hear it.

Contact Heather on "Stoke Your Fire Within" via Facebook,
Website: www.heatherstoker.com,
Email: stokeyourfirewithin@gmail.com.
Literary Manager: Ken Eulo with KMA

CPSIA information can be obtained
at www.ICGtesting.com
Printed in the USA
LVHW081502230122
709163LV00011B/336

9 781953 114037